BREADCRUMBS

Finding a Philosophy of Life

WILLIAM F. MERCK II

BREADCRUMBS

Finding a Philosophy of Life

WILLIAM F. MERCK II

MII

MERCK II PRESS

FOR KSENIA

Contents

Preface

IN MY SOPHOMORE YEAR OF COLLEGE, one of my professors asked his students about their personal philosophy of life. He was a sociology teacher who preferred to be addressed as *Major* Grant. That title, presumably from some vague military experience, complemented the superior attitude he kept on display, as he strutted around the front of his classroom. When he asked that question one day during a lecture—after sharing a few of his non-memorable thoughts on his place in life—I stirred from my boredom and thought, *I'm eighteen years old. I haven't lived long enough to answer that.*

Sometimes, very thought-provoking questions come from the unlikeliest sources, and this was certainly one of those instances. The "Major" was hardly a philosopher nor a deep thinker. Still, I've thought about that professor's question many times since. Now that I have lived longer and accumulated some experience in life, I have an answer. Occasionally, I bring up this question with others and ask them to sum up their life philosophies in a sentence. But how anyone sees life is complex and can rarely be expressed in an answer that fits on a bumper sticker. My views on life cannot be summarized in one sentence. They demand a longer answer that has roots in my childhood experiences, my views on religion, prejudice, nature, war, the development of character, and, ultimately, the enlightenment that comes from reflection on what all these experiences have to do with shaping who I am.

Where do my thoughts come from?

Why do I feel certain ways about people?

Why am I here?

What makes me special or different?

How do I know if something is right or wrong?

Is there a power greater than me?

Do I have a purpose to fulfill?

Why do I prefer one thing over another?

When did I form that opinion?

Do I have an obligation to society?

Various religions attempt to answer these types of questions to explain our value and existence. Philosophical icons in history have offered deep and thoughtful dissertations. But, in the end, it is up to the individual, should they so desire, to seek an understanding of the motivations behind the development of their own beliefs as to why they are here and what they should do with the infinite possibilities this life gives to them—a life given that probabilities suggest never should have occurred. Each person choosing to articulate how they view the world and their place in it, or what I'm calling "finding a philosophy of life," will see their core beliefs shaped by a lifetime of unique experiences.

In the following pages, I use my life's experiences to show how they shaped my view of the world, forming my personal philosophy of life. At times, when something new slapped me in the face, the shock transformed an earlier view, and I was completely aware of what had just happened. Other times, a less traumatic, transformational event happened, and it took decades for me to fully understand the impact that event had on my way of thinking. This delay in attributing cause to the effect was particularly true of experiences in my youth when my reasoning ability was limited in experience. I had no basis for contrast or comparison. An example of a delayed understanding that occurred early in my life was being around creative, innovative people. I absorbed their abstract ways of thinking without realizing what fortunate gifts they were until many years later.

Who I am has a great deal to do with the influences of my early experiences. Who was I around then? What did these people believe? How readily did I absorb and adopt their views, setting me on a path for what I might become? As powerful as childhood influences are—and they are powerful—I now realize I have the capacity to alter any path they might have set me on, guided by my later, more mature experiences, if I choose to do so. If I refuse to allow myself to succumb to a state of emotional and intellectual calcification along the way, I will learn, grow, and reach my full potential as a human being. I know introspection, no matter how messy or uncomfortable it might make me feel at times, will allow me to develop a deeper and richer philosophy of life.

Likewise, you have your own set of life events that have shaped who you are and how you see the world. You are as unique as a snowflake; among others, you appear very much alike but when viewed up close, you are all different. The path of your life starts with your early childhood experiences, which includes the people in those experiences and the physical environment in which those events occurred. I invite you to consider the influences on your life as I share some of my early experiences and discoveries.

In this work, I use stories from my life's journey to illustrate points that shape my view of the world and my place in it. The names of some people have been obscured when warranted. I loosely base the book's framework on the seven philosophies of education and concentrate on themes of learning, values, reasoning, morals, religion, aesthetics, and world views. These are my breadcrumbs.

‑‑⁄ı\‑

Learning and Understanding

CHILDHOOD INFLUENCES

Lying on a bed of leaves atop a grape arbor I had been forbidden to climb, looking up at the clear blue sky on an early fall morning and savoring my secret rebellion against authority, I reached out and plucked a ripe scuppernong grape, put it in my mouth, squeezed out the sweet juice, and spit the seeds into the air, not concerned about where they would fall. Oh, the life of a five-year-old.

The environment surrounding a child in the first few years of life have a profound effect on their development as a human being. The people, particularly adults, and the physical surroundings of a young child are what form their only world. Community and surroundings shape early perceptions of what life is all about.

Most of my life lessons were certainly imparted to me this way. Remembering these times illustrate cause and effect in how life is understood and profoundly shaped. My stories are not intended to imply that what I experienced is typical. Since each childhood is unique, adult perceptions are, in the same sense, unique, as they were influenced by each person's different childhood environment. My childhood experiences are not typical because they occurred in a particular time and place, with specific people at that time and place. That's what makes my experiences one-of-a-kind, just as yours are.

I am fortunate that I had a peaceful existence as a child. Many lives have foundations set in worn-torn countries. A few in recent generations include Vietnam, Cambodia, Sudan, Syria, and Ukraine. Some children are traumatized throughout early life in rough neighborhoods. These are not war-torn countries, but areas controlled by drug cartels or gangs who terrorize families living in fear of crossing them. In these environments, children lose their families to violence. Too many, unfortunately, watch their parents and siblings being killed. These profound influences on a child have enormous implications for the direction their lives take going forward. In some cases, these traumatic circumstances may cause the survivors to push themselves toward achievements they would not otherwise have attempted.

In other cases, the disruption in education, nutrition, and medical care—added to the psychological stresses—cause a severe lessening of a life that could have been. I speculate on these circumstances, from the outside looking in. So, to have confidence in my observations about the formation of a philosophy of life, or my view of the world, I rely on my own experiences and the experiences of others that I have seen first-hand and relate how those experiences shaped my view.

That morning long ago, lying on my back after climbing to the top of my grandfather's grape arbor, gave me an overwhelming sense of peace and joy to be alive. As I looked up at the beauty of the vast blue sky, with air so clear it was a pleasure to breathe, I believe that may have been my first conscious appreciation of the true beauty of nature. I watched white clouds floating overhead, while noticing the sensation on my skin of the cool fall air tempered by the warmth of the sun. Add to this the pleasure of the sweet taste of the ripe grapes I casually plucked from the ancient vine springing from the earth beneath me, and it is no wonder that memory is still so vivid in my consciousness.

This memory was formed while my parents and I lived with my maternal grandparents, Lowry and Alma Keefe, in their house in the rural setting of Jamestown, near the small South Georgia town of Waycross. I was born in October 1944, about seven months before the end of World War II in Europe. My brother, Lowry, was born about five years after me. My two other brothers came later, David, ten years after me, and Jeffrey, born a little more than a year after David. My father was overseas and in the army during part of my first year alive. When he returned to civilian life, we lived in Jamestown until I was five.

As the first grandchild, I received a lot of attention from my grandparents and from an aunt and uncle, Gerri and Ernie, who lived nearby for a time. Some of the vibrant memories I have resulted from the proximity to these family members, observing their daily actions and interactions, and participating in their activities to the extent I could as a toddler and then a pre-school youngster.

The late-1940s for my family were a time of new beginnings, leaving behind the Great Depression and the strenuous war years. My dad was starting a new job, my grandfather was transitioning from full time work to retirement, and my mom and grandmother were taking care of all the household chores. In those days, that meant washing clothes without a washer and dryer, boiling soiled diapers in a big cast iron kettle in the backyard, canning fruits and vegetables, cooking everything from scratch, keeping things clean, and, of course, taking care of me. I do remember it as a good time, and why not? They were doing all the work, and I was enjoying the good life.

In those early times, I made friends with a girl who lived about a half mile away. One Saturday at her house, she suggested we make a little lake in a large baking dish. We used the hand pump in her kitchen sink to get water from the well to put in the dish. We used half eggshells to use as boats floating on our lake. She added blue ink to the water, which struck me at the time as such a clever idea to use ink made for writing to color our pond. What a genius she was! We cut pictures of people from a Sears, Roebuck and Co. catalog to put in the boats, gluing them upright on toothpicks. We put something in the bottom of the eggshells to act as ballasts to keep them upright. Bunches of grass from the yard floated on the lake to simulate islands. It was quite a fun day and a great experience. My friend opened my eyes to seeing how ordinary items can be transformed into something very special with imagination and creativity.

Occasionally, on a Saturday, my dad would take me with him to the local icehouse to buy a big block of ice to break up and use in our ice cream churn he set up in the backyard. I still remember the taste of the strawberry ice cream that we made. Delicious. I also watched my dad and grandfather pick grapes from the arbor to make wine. They designed and built a raised tub to crush the grapes, which was attached to a wooden trough made from two pieces of lumber fastened together in a "V" shape to drain the juice from the tub into a container, with the juice now separated from the must that contains the skins, seeds, and stems of the grapes. They poured the filtered juice into large jugs they had painted white to protect the liquid from light while it fermented. Then, all the jugs went into an outbuilding called a smokehouse, which they had converted from the purpose of smoking meat to a storage building.

After a time, the juice turned to wine through a process I couldn't fathom as a kid. These were experiences watching the adults in my life create the means to an end, with good humor and excellent skills. Like my friend impressing me with her creative skills in forming a lake in a baking dish, I was again absorbing a way of thinking about my surroundings, adding to a developing reservoir of imagination and creativity.

In the earlier of those first five years of my life, my grandfather worked as a painter in the Charleston, South Carolina, naval shipyard, painting warships and submarines. A combat veteran of World War I, he was past the age to serve in World War II, but he still found a way to help as a civilian working in the Charleston shipyard. I picked up enough from offhand comments or small details in stories he told to know that he was involved in some counter-sabotage work for the government in addition to his work as a painter. One encounter he shared involved a saboteur working undercover in the shipyard who was attempting to disable a warship.

It was crucial that warships that came into port for maintenance or repair from war damage were there for a very short time so they could get back into service. When a ship was in port, and, therefore, out of action, sabotage could extend to that downtime in port. What Grandfather mentioned in his story concerned a suspicious man inserting small metal shims in key runs of a ship's electric wiring. The saboteur's plan was to short out portions of the circuitry critical to the ship's functions. These shorts would only become evident after the repairs and maintenance were completed, and the ship was launched back into the sea under full power. The saboteur's desired result was to force the ship to return to port so it would be out of action for more time. I know my grandfather was responsible for foiling that particular plot. I was intrigued by this aspect of his personality and began to grasp that people are often much more than they seem to be on the surface.

During his time working in Charleston, he would come home by train early on Saturday mornings and then leave again late on Sunday nights. In those days, men wore suits and dress hats to travel. He would arrive from the train station looking very fine in his gray suit and Fedora hat, sporting a gold chain attached to the watch that ticked away the time in his vest pocket. He was always happy to see us. As a ritual, he would bring me a small cigar box containing pennies when he came home. Since at that age I wasn't great at counting, I'm guessing the boxes contained about fifty pennies each time. Overjoyed, in my eyes it was a box full of treasure. I'm confident I could not fully absorb the meaning at the time, but the fact that I knew he spent the week in some mysterious, faraway place, returning home on weekends, gave me a vague sense that the world was much bigger than my familiar child's environment.

Across the country road in front of our house was a railroad that was used quite frequently. Nights in bed, I would listen to the sound of the train clattering by on the tracks and the soulful sounds of warning coming from the whistle as it approached road crossings. For some reason, it was a peaceful sound to me. Probably because when I heard it, I was tucked into a warm, safe bed with nothing to be afraid of, and that was the association. During the day, one of our pastimes was to count the freight cars as they passed, and I would sometimes wonder what they were carrying and where they might be going. My parents instilled a deep sense of caution in me about the dangers of being near the tracks when a train might be coming, but at that age, it was not really a problem, since I never went near them alone.

I did hear stories of people putting a penny on the tracks to have them flattened by the heavy rolling train. Dad warned me not to ever place anything on the tracks, as it might cause a derailment. We didn't get into the specifics of how that might work but it brought me a sense of awareness around the lesson of cause and consequence, even though I didn't know those words at the time. Growing up in the proximity of a railroad and seeing trains on a regular basis infused me with a growing sense that these trains were a means I might someday use to travel to exciting places I could only dream of.

In this same bedroom where I slept and fantasized about train travel was an old radio, one of those three-foot-high contraptions with large speakers at the bottom and two analog dials at the top. Under the dials lay a row of push buttons that no longer worked; the purpose of these controls in earlier days were for tuning into preset stations. The reception of the radio was limited to local stations that I could get by carefully dialing in one of the knobs to the exact frequency.

One day, I decided to attempt to extend the range by running an extra wire. I attached it to the antenna I found on the back of the set, threaded it through my bedroom window, and affixed it to the metal rain gutter that ran around the eaves of the entire house. My expectations were surpassed when I turned on the set and began to receive programs spoken in a foreign language! My imagination went wild thinking about the foreign lands I was tapping into, lands that someday I might travel to. From Southern Georgia, I was actually picking up Cuban stations several hundred miles to the south. But at that time to me, it seemed like much more.

Finally, my dreams of exotic travel by train materialized when I was allowed as an eleven-year-old to ride on a train, unaccompanied, to visit my aunt and uncle in Atlanta, some 250 miles away. The trip was as exciting as I had hoped it would be. At times, I stood in the connection way between the passenger cars and exuberantly stuck my head and shoulders out of the opening, in the top half of the door, into the wind!

While in Atlanta several years later as a college student, I met Bob Daniels. At that time, he was the art director for *Atlanta* magazine and was preparing an article on The General, the locomotive involved in the historic Great Locomotive Chase that occurred in 1862 during the Civil War. The story he was writing included a photo shoot of The General, which had been taken out of museum storage and loaded onto railroad tracks near Atlanta. After workers got it underway, a photographer raced beside it while driving along a parallel highway, stopping several times ahead of the train's progress to take action shots.

The cool thing for me was when Bob invited me along for the ride. I was able to experience what it was like to be in a historic passenger car pulled by The General. My childhood interest in trains undoubtedly had something to do with my conversations with the director leading up to the invitation. As with so many steps on the trail of life's breadcrumbs, I know there was a connection.

DEVELOPING CURIOSITY

I started the first grade when I was five. The school was a two-room, white clapboard structure with unheated bathrooms attached to the back of the building. I remember the wooden floor in the bathroom. I could see the ground about two feet below me, through cracks between the floorboards, cracks that the winter wind would whistle up through. One classroom in the building was for the first grade; the second and third grade classes shared the other one. The main school for the upper grades was separated from our small building by railroad tracks, flanked on either side by drainage swales, and then a highway. The lunchroom we shared was attached to the main part of the school. When we made our daily trek over for lunch, the last obstacle after the railroad tracks and the highway was a fence around the lunch yard. We accessed the yard by using a set of wooden steps, called a pig style, to climb up and over that fence that kept out pigs and cows. Livestock wasn't required to be confined to pastures in those days, but instead roamed freely.

While this all seemed, and actually was, rather primitive, I liked the kids, and the first-grade teacher I had was excellent! She really went above and beyond when my second dog, a Fox Terrier, was killed crossing the highway in front of our house. I was heartbroken. Dad came home from work; we made a small coffin and buried the dog in the yard with a wooden cross, painted silver, marking the site. Knowing how badly I felt, within a week of the accident, my teacher gave me a new mixed breed, primarily Cocker Spaniel, puppy. She was a strict disciplinarian but had a good heart and a real empathy for her students. That teacher was one of the best role models I had in my years as a student. I'm fortunate that she was my first impression of a teacher.

The dog that was killed I had named Riley. I penciled in his name in our family Bible, an act that upset my father to no end. He angrily erased the name and asked me what would have happened if we were all killed in some accident. What then if someone looked in our Bible and saw all our names, and Riley was included? People would be looking for another kid in our family named Riley! I guess I understood. However, Riley was a pal in those days. Every Thursday afternoon at four, Riley and I sat in one of the large chairs in our living room and listened to the big radio that sat there before it was moved into my bedroom, broadcasting another story in the *Lone Ranger* series. I'm not sure Riley appreciated the stories, but he was a good sport sitting with me for a half hour while I listened. One afternoon, we knelt on the dirt in the chicken yard and shared a snack of laying mash in a wooden trough meant for the chickens. That was a shared event I think he enjoyed much more than listening to the Lone Ranger with me. Having that relationship with Riley was important in seeing how animals have their own personalities and are individuals in their own right. He had an influence on how I understood many other animals in my life after that time.

When work at the naval yard slowed down after the war, Grandfather retired and returned full time to being with the family. The house we all lived in was one he built in the 1930s and situated on about five acres of land in the Jamestown countryside. It had two coal-burning space heaters: one in the dining room and one in a large back room that was adjacent to the kitchen and a bedroom. In the early fall, a dump truck would come and drop a huge load of anthracite coal on the property that would last for the winter; that was the fuel used to heat the house. It was not my regular chore, but, occasionally, I would march out into the cold carrying a coalscuttle to the big pile and proudly bring in a load of coal pieces for the fires. This was a way for me to contribute to the activities of the family and feel a part of it.

Grandfather raised chickens and had fruit trees and a vegetable garden. On about four of his five acres, he planted in corn. The sight of him in his field was remarkable: I watched him preparing the soil for planting, on foot in the freshly plowed furrows, grasping the wooden handles of a big plow, reins over his neck and shoulders, and following the mule that pulled that plow churning up the soil. When I saw him working in his garden or field, he was always clothed from head to toe. Long pants, a long-sleeved shirt, and a large brimmed straw hat covered his body. His face and hands were tanned, but nowhere else. He was not an exception for his generation. Women working outside were similarly covered, wearing dresses down to their ankles, long-sleeved blouses, and full sun hats. To be sure, it was uncomfortably hot in the Southern summers working outdoors, but the head-to-toe clothing sheltering the skin from the sun was never sacrificed to gain comfort from the heat.

In those days, rural folks working their fields understood the need to protect themselves from the damaging rays of the sun. However, that innate understanding was lost on the next generation, who found pleasure dressed in skimpy swimwear, lying on beaches or poolside while baking their exposed bodies to achieve a coveted "tan." Many sunbathers would lather themselves with baby oil to presumably help the tanning process. I have jokingly compared that process to basting a Thanksgiving turkey with juices while it cooked over a hot charcoal grill. It was only later that commercial sunscreens came into popular use. But given their intermittent application, I wonder how much good they actually did in the long term.

I never heard of anyone in my grandparents' generation suffering from skin cancer. That certainly changed, as more of the next generation began to spend time in the sun without the protective coverings of their forbearers. I must admit to being of that naïve generation. As a kid, my attire in the warm seasons was simply a pair of shorts and sandals. In my pre-teen and teen years, I spent considerable time outdoors with no hat and, for a time, worked as a lifeguard at a pool. Sun damage to skin is a cumulative affair. I certainly accumulated my share, and more, of sun damage, causing me to deal with the removal of various skin cancers in my later years. My grandparents never owned a pair of shorts. On the one or two occasions I saw my grandfather in sandals, he wore them with socks, having no concern as to the unfashionable statement he made. Dad sometimes wore shorts, but typically only on weekends. Mother wore shorts more often than he did, which was a contrast to my grandmother, who never did.

Times were changing. But in my generation, we ran around wearing shorts and short-sleeved shirts, with no hats, and spent leisure hours basking in the sun. It was a lifestyle that started in my childhood. I wouldn't change any of this time spent in the sun, but skin cancer is certainly a downside. I see this as one of the many tradeoffs in life I have faced where I decided to choose something that gives pleasure, knowing there will be a downside that I will own. In my life, I try to anticipate the worst that can happen when I make one of these choices of pleasure over potentially bad consequences. Being mindful of the choice and the consequence—and then, with that internal understanding, deliberately making the choice—has helped me avoid regret or guilt over some of the bad outcomes I've endured.

Life is full of dings, cuts, and abuse suffered by our bodies. When someone is hurt, I have several times heard the pitiful cry, "Why me? What did I do to deserve this?" My unspoken response is, "Why not you?" I learned early on that I was not immune to cuts, bruises, and broken bones, and have had countless stitches patching me up over the years. That is just the way it is. I had pneumonia when I was two. Doctors made house calls in the 1940s, so our family physician came by to treat me as best he could. Mother told me later, after the doctor left our house, that he said I had a fifty-fifty chance of living through the night. Among others, Uncle Ernie stayed with me all through that critical night. A devout Catholic, he hung a Saint Sebastian medal on a chain on the bedpost, a medal my wife and I have to this day.

Needless to say, I did survive. That same doctor came to see me when I was a bit older, following an incident where I had somehow stuck a rusty nail right on a blood vein just above my wrist. Blood poisoning had set in, and a red streak was starting to run up my arm. The doctor said that if we allowed the red streak, indicating the progress of the infection, to reach my heart, it would be all over for me. He directed me to keep my arm from the elbow to my hand immersed in hot water, infused with Epsom salts, to slow and stop the spread. Believe me, I was all about keeping the water hot and my arm immersed! It must have worked because the progress of the red streak stopped, and the death line faded away.

Another time, he sewed my scalp together after a situation when I was using both hands and my arms to hammer a nail in a board. On the upswing, I managed to drive the claw end of the hammer into the top of my head, leaving a bloody cut. I have incorporated the understanding in my view of the world that accidents will happen, and pain will ensue. The awareness that accidents I can't anticipate is something I accept as a given; I do not let that awareness give me cause for useless worry.

In more recent days, I ripped up the ligaments in my left foot in an accident. Wearing a "boot" to give support during the healing weeks gave me a personal understanding of what disabled people confront in their daily lives. Mine was temporary; for others, their disability is permanent. It is certainly revealing to go through routine activities before a physical setback, day after day, and not give them a second thought until they become major efforts to accomplish. And additionally, to be forced to understand how daily physical pain accompanies these efforts. My car has a manual transmission. Overnight, it became impossible for me to drive because I was unable to manage the clutch wearing the big boot. A big part of my independence gone!

Climbing stairs became a strenuous and time-consuming affair. Changing planes in an airport with tight turnaround times became quite challenging. Simple tasks around the house, like cleaning leaves from a gutter, become a high-risk undertaking, so I chose to no longer attempt them. Many activities I did before, I now had to rely on others for their help. I have learned from some of my injuries how fortunate I have been that they were not permanently disabling. I know that these events have helped me become more understanding of the special efforts required in everyday life for those who have their abilities compromised in some way. As a result, I am more observant of opportunities to offer assistance when it may be needed and accepted by others.

Any given mental state is just as susceptible to dings and bruises as the body, but these injuries often take longer to repair. There are choices in life. Sometimes, the results of bad choices are haunting. Imperfect humans make bad choices from time to time. How much time it will take to heal any mental aftermath is directly connected to how I choose to deal with it. My mother used to tell me that she did not worry about things she had no control over. She just worried about what she could control. I try to apply this bit of wisdom to mental healing in this way: I cannot change the past, what I have done, or what bad decisions I may have made. I cannot go back in time and change any of it. What I can do is try to learn from my mistakes and use that knowledge to influence my actions and decisions in the future. I can control that.

There is a "but" to this statement in that I do not always have complete control over what my mind focuses on or tells me to do. Being distracted, sleep-deprived, or any number of other reasons will cause me to lose an iron grip on controlling my thoughts. That is just the way it is. What I can do, however, in the aftermath of a bad decision is limit my time agonizing, recognize my frailties as a human, and move on to focusing on the future. I worked with a woman once who said when something bad happens to her, she allows herself two days to feel sorry for herself. After that, she moves on. I do the best I can.

My grandmother worked part-time for our family doctor during the early years of my life. I thought she was a nurse but later understood her medical training was all on the job. However, in the very few times when I was sick, she would bring home from her stint with the doctor a syringe of penicillin and give me a shot. When I had ringworm on my knees from playing in the dirt, she would bring home a canister of liquid nitrogen and spray the infected area, clearing it up. I never had to show her any proof of insurance, and she didn't require me to sign indemnity waivers!

In our kitchen cutlery drawers, I would see her collection of stainless-steel surgical knives for cutting meat and a surgical bone saw she used to cut the bones in roasts or hams. At a young age, I began to appreciate the value of medical practitioners. I was learning that when I became physically damaged from time to time, there were doctors and hospitals to attend to me and painful as each of the instances might be, the world would not end because of it. The use of dichloro-diphenyl-trichloroethane, or DDT, began in the 1940s as an agricultural pesticide. Grandfather would come in from a hot day working his field, his clothing drenched in sweat, and his whole body ghostly white, covered with the DDT he had been spreading over his crop. We had no idea in those days of the dangers posed by exposure to that compound. He died in his eighties from cancer. Who knows what the effects of DDT, the lead paints and solvents he used in his painting career, or the other chemicals he was exposed to while fighting in trench warfare with mustard and chlorine gases had on his body over time. Even though I mention the wartime exposure, I don't suspect the gases in World War I had much effect, as those exposures usually resulted in immediate permanent disability or death.

Hearing my grandfather's stories of the deadly use of chlorine and mustard gases gave me a morbid curiosity about those terrible weapons. This curiosity was satisfied through an experience I had during my high school years when I worked a few summers for the city recreation department. One of my lifeguard duties on alternate Saturday mornings was to clean the pool filter and check for leaks in the fittings that attached chlorine gas canisters to the pool's pumping system. This gas was used to purify the pool water. Checking for leaks involved using a swab from a small bottle of a liquid chemical that would emit smoke if placed in the vicinity of chlorine gas.

So, on my days to perform the maintenance chores, I would dutifully rub the swab around all of the fittings, always wondering if this test would actually work. But to my surprise, one morning I got smoke! So, being stupid, but curious, I began to wonder what the deadly chlorine gas I had heard so much about in my grandfather's wartime stories was like. I rationalized that in such a small quantity as was leaking from the canister's fitting, surely it would not be deadly. But maybe it was still enough to let me know what it was like. I positioned myself at the open door to the cramped pool house so that if something bad happened, I would fall outside into the clean air. Then, I cautiously leaned over the leaking fitting and took a little whiff. Oh my, that infinitely small exposure felt like I had shot a dose of Clorox right into my nostrils. It was unbelievably painful! As I immediately pulled away, the pain slowly cleared, and I learned how powerful even a very small, invisible sniff of that gas is. My curiosity was satisfied.

THE IMPACT OF EXERCISE

WHEN I WAS YOUNG AND ACTIVE, I didn't spend much time worrying about exercise. But when I become older and my physical activities waned, I realized I needed to do more. That doesn't mean I actually did more, but I did spend more time thinking about it. For most kids, there is a lot of time spent in motion, as the body grows into maturity. The range and frequency of that movement has a lot to do with building ultimate strength and durability throughout life. Many of my youthful activities involved running, climbing, biking, swimming, and walking. These, with maybe the exception of swimming, are not unusual activities while growing up. The important factors are frequency and diversity of movement.

In my earliest years, I played outside with my dogs Dance and, later, Riley. The trees on the property were perfect for climbing. I had a tricycle and a swing set. Other kids I grew up with were similarly active in their youth. We didn't have televisions or computers, so there was not any enticement to stay inside to entertain ourselves. The outdoors was where the action was, "action" being a key word. Learning to swim early in life, physically paddling wooden fishing boats on the St. Marys River, walking miles through the woods, riding horses, and other activities had very positive effects on developing my young body. Grade school involved walking to school every day. I was fairly coordinated but not particularly athletically skilled. I tried out for all the typical sports: track, baseball, football, and basketball. I found that I was not particularly good at any of them, but I did enjoy basketball and tennis. I started basketball in the fourth grade, and I showed up on my first day of practice wearing cowboy boots. My coach suggested I get more appropriate footwear. I was assigned to whatever was the lowest string until, during my ninth-grade year, I decided rather than go to practice every day but not be allowed to play in the games, I would start my own team in the city recreation center league so I could play in every game every week. That turned out to be great fun. However, by late into my tenth-grade year, my best friends in high school were the guys on the school's basketball team. They were extremely talented. They knew I had left the team because I could not compete at their level but since we were all friends, they arranged for me to travel on the team bus with them to all the away games and to be present at the home events to keep the game records.

One friend, Larry Harrison, became my college roommate. He was good enough to play on our college team. I also kept the game stats for the high school baseball team one year for similar reasons. In my sophomore year in college, I played tennis on the college team; I did letter in the sport. However, at the year's end, when the athletic director was giving out the letters to the team, I think he had a moment's hesitation in handing over mine, since I had never won a match in competition with other schools. Oh well.

My work at the city recreation center in high school was that of a lifeguard. That position also meant I was required to participate in the annual summer water show put on for the community. I did enjoy it, as did everyone who joined. Participation involved learning synchronized swimming, which comprised a good portion of the show's acts. One of the acts I was in was a synchronized duet—meaning there was only me and my female partner in the pool, under the spotlights, performing on show nights for a local crowd. The guy that had the part the year before me in that duet was nicknamed "Triceps," if that gives you an idea of his physique. The final act of the duet performance involved Triceps lifting his young partner over his head, while she was stretched out in the air above him in a graceful, horizontal pose, and holding her there as the music came to a crescendo. Okay, so the next summer, when

I was a senior and it was my act to perform, the director took one look at my arms and decided I was to lift my partner in her graceful pose just up to my waist in the water and hold her there. I was a little embarrassed by the change in the script ... but highly relieved!

During these years, I was also into running several times a week to stay in shape. All of that preceded my three years after college in the military. As a result, the physical part of military training was challenging but not overly difficult for me. In fact, I earned the highest score in one of our company's physical fitness tests. It's clear to me that a variety of activity in my younger days paid off in terms of my physical well-being later in life. While I missed the accolades of being a skilled athlete, which I was certainly not, the running, cycling, swimming, and climbing associated with varied physical activity in my younger years became important in what I was able to achieve later. Absent extenuating circumstances, medical conditions, or injury, a young person's physical activity correlates positively with the physical condition of the adult.

TOUCHING THE HOT STOVE

METAPHORICALLY, IF NOT LITERALLY, CHILDREN WILL touch a hot stove to see if it really is as hot as they are warned. Maybe we never quite grow out of that curiosity to test harmful things we are warned about, just as I had done with the chlorine gas. In a counterintuitive sense, this innate curiosity is sometimes a positive attribute because some of the bad stuff we are warned about is not actually bad—just misunderstood, taken out of context, or vilified for some nefarious purpose. For example, the belief in witches led to many people being identified as such and subsequently killed. In colonial Massachusetts, the Salem Witch Trials, held between 1692 and 1693, were a notable example in America. In Europe, from the 1300s to the end of the 1600s, there was a sort of witchcraft craze, and tens of thousands of people—mostly women—were executed for being witches. Some "bad" things we are warned about, like the reality of witches, really should be questioned. There was incalculable harm to innocent, but misunderstood, folks. All this might have been avoided by having sufficient curiosity to rationally question things that have been mislabeled for unknown reasons—and this applies to much more than just witches!

Influential people in positions of power create false narratives about groups of people they wish to subjugate. One tactic is to attribute an undesirable trait, true or not, to the targeted population. The trait in the narrative does not need to be real if the spin-masters involved are adept at manipulating public opinion. While there is generally a seed of truth involved to make such outrageous ideas go viral, it behooves people to be curious about odd declarations and seek to understand the true motivations and objectives behind them. Unfortunately, many people don't. Some stoves should be touched to see if they really are hot.

There seems to be a relationship between risk-taking in youth and tolerance for risk as an adult. Childhood is a time where many risks are taken, and while some can seem pretty scary at the time, in reality, the consequences of a bad outcome are not on the magnitude of failure in the higher-stakes outcomes of many adult decisions. My hypothesis is that risks taken early in life can have an effect on my later tolerance for making decisions that involve risk with meaningful consequences. A simple example is a decision about taking on a mortgage to purchase a house. The two big variables to weigh are the cost of the house, in relation to my financial resources, and my comfort level with the resulting monthly mortgage payments. A rational assessment of the best decision is often clouded by emotion. Personal experience with risk plays a role in the weight, given the emotional side of the scale. This comes down to reason versus emotion. How much experience in situations involving risk do I have? Did those experiences have acceptable outcomes, or is there a greater history of failure? Knowing this makes a difference. I heard an adage years ago that stuck with me: "Emotion is the river upon which logic floats."

There are some childhood experiences that are relevant to developing a tolerance for risk at an early age. A few of these are unique to me, but, in general, they are the type of experiences children go through that can help them face risks later in life when the stakes are larger. For example, playing with marbles taught me something. You know the game; a circle is drawn in the dirt and the players place their equal share of marbles in the center. Each person gets a turn as the "shooter," usually using a marble they believe works best for this purpose. One kid in our group used a metal ball bearing as his shooter. I was not sure if that was within the rules, and I challenged its use. But the other kids allowed that it was okay.

During some games, we would play for keeps. This meant that whatever marbles you were able to knock out of the circle when it was your turn to shoot, you kept. We would play until all the marbles were gone from the circle. This may have been one of the first times I was confronted with the concept of risking an asset I owned by choosing to participate in an activity. And lose some of my marbles I did, but I also won some of the other players' marbles.

At the end of a game, I would assess whether I came out ahead, not only in the net count of my gain or loss but in the quality of the marbles I won versus those I lost. As a quality metric, cat's eye marbles were particularly coveted.

A variation on this lesson came when some of us decided to trade one of our toys for another kid's toy. I once traded a realistic-looking rubber knife in a sheath for another boy's replica of a miniature Native American birchbark canoe. After the trade, I suffered what I later understood to be buyer's remorse. We would trade comic books as well, but since they were so similar in substance, that didn't affect me like trading dissimilar toys. That first trade for the little canoe influenced my later thinking about trades. I learned not to act on impulse but to carefully weigh the pros and cons of a trade before making a decision. I'm thankful I learned this lesson at an early age.

There was a boy, Larry, who lived not too far away that I sometimes played with. One afternoon, we were at my house when we were about four years old. I had this idea, from where I don't know, that if we walked down the road from my house and kept turning right at each crossroad, we would end up back at my house. This was sort of like walking around the block, even though I didn't know what a block was. I also had no idea how far this walk would be, living in the country. Well, we walked and walked. About two thirds of the way into our adventure, we came upon a cow in our path. I was somewhat familiar with cows, so I thought it was no big deal as we made our way, running, around the cow. Larry was frightened of the cow, to the point he burst into tears from fear. His house came first as we finished our journey, and he left me to go on to my house, which was a little farther down the road.

By the time I arrived home, Larry had tried to explain to his mother what took place on our outing, why it had taken way more time than he had anticipated, and that it was all my idea. He tearfully told her we were lost and had almost been eaten by a cow. She called my mother, quite upset, berating her for what I had talked her little boy into and the dangers involved. I was in trouble when I got home, but I didn't understand the big deal being made of our adventure. Though I didn't think of it in these terms, I took a risk for the thrill of an adventure. The trouble I got into for that action did not, even then, outweigh the pleasure of the excitement I got from the experience.

Larry's mother was missing half of one of her thumbs, and one day, I asked about what had happened. Her story relates to the way most of the families I knew prepared ground meat for cooking. The piece of kitchen equipment used for that purpose was about eighteen inches high, with a clamp on the bottom that was temporarily fixed to the edge of a kitchen counter or a tabletop to provide stability. The top of the piece was funnel-shaped, with a hand crank on the side to turn blades in the device that ground the meat when pushed into the funnel. When the meat passed through the device after being ground, it exited from a side hole into a bowl. When my neighbor was turning the crank with one hand, she was forcefully pushing a piece of meat with the other hand down into the funnel that led to the blades. She pushed too hard and far, and her thumb hit the blades and was cut off before she stopped turning the crank. This was an early lesson regarding care when working with tools of all kinds.

In the summer months, my parents would take me to pick blackberries that grew wild on the fencerow separating my grandfather's field from the lane that ran beside it. The blackberries were plentiful and good for making cobbler. I was cautioned to watch for snakes in the bushes, as they would climb in there to catch a bird that had landed to eat some berries. I never saw one, but the idea of being aware of potential dangers while in the outdoors was ingrained in me. The risk of snakebite while picking berries was obviously weighed to a point, but it was found not to override the joy of picking the berries. This experience was one of many that led to the understanding that nature is an environment that is at once beautiful and peaceful as well as dangerous and terrifying. Understanding how nature exists with both predators and prey, with elements that sustain one form of life but are deadly to others, is necessary for success living in nature. Knowing the differences— having awareness of the relationships between living things in the wild and human life—is imperative, not only for survival as a minimum but for obtaining a joy in living and optimizing the use of resources available in nature to sustain body and soul.

Climbing trees was a big thing when I was four and five years old. One of the trees in the yard was a very tall magnolia. A couple of times, when the sky would grow dark and the wind would fiercely blow just before a storm struck, I would climb to the top of the tree and hang on while the top blew back and forth. The feeling of the wind blowing across my body and in my face and the sound of the leaves straining against the wind was positively euphoric. I believe the definite feeling of euphoria I experienced was caused by the negative ions created in the air by the storm front moving in, along with the excitement of hanging on to the blowing treetop. By the way, my mother was unaware of what I was doing, and I decided not to share.

As I got a little older, there were other times I engaged in risky behavior and the results were okay, but the outcomes were determined by luck rather than good judgment. The following are three examples.

Swimming in the St. Marys River near Charlie and Georgia Merck's house, my paternal grandparents, was quite different from swimming in a conventional pool. The water was dark brown, almost black, from the tannic acid released from tree roots and swamp vegetation fringing the river. While dark, it was very clean and safe to drink. And the darkness made it great for games of hide-and-seek because when we went underwater, we disappeared. Grandfather Merck had several wooden boats tied to his dock that we would swim around and under as part of the game. Of course, before we went in for the swim, we would first check for any water snakes that might be hanging around. Occasionally, there would be some, and we would undertake different measures to get rid of them.

On one of these times, I went down to his dock. At the end was a square deck, balanced on several steel barrels so that it would "float" or raise and lower with the water level as the tides changed. The wooden structure underneath, which held everything together, was surrounded on the outer edges with skirt boards, leaving about eight inches from the bottom of the boards to the water. During my snake check of the area, I leaned over the edge and looked under the deck. Sure enough, there was a big snake lying there in the dim light on one of the boards. I ran up to the house, retrieved Grandfather's .22 caliber rifle, and came back down. I quietly slid into the water, holding the rifle over my head to keep it dry, and ducked under the eight-inch opening popping up under the deck.

Taking a quick but poor aim, I shot the snake. Then the stupidity of the whole undertaking hit me. The big snake, only wounded, dropped into the black water. Here I was, just a few feet from a hurt snake joining me in the water, where I could no longer see him, and now I had to go underwater to get back out from under the floating dock. I was able to escape. I know there must be a lesson in that experience. I'm still thinking about how to benefit from it in other life situations. Maybe it's as simple as not voluntarily exposing oneself to dangerous situations having little to no gain and with questionable control over the outcome.

The riverbed near the shoreline gradually sloped down as one waded out until it was too deep to stand. Then a little further on, the slope began a sharp decent to the river bottom toward the middle, where it was about fifty feet deep. We referred to that demarcation line between shallow water and deep as the "drop-off." Because of the depth of St. Marys, it was locally known during World War II that an occasional German U-Boat would navigate that far up the river from the ocean to restock their supply of fresh water. One afternoon, when I was about twelve or thirteen, a boy my age, the son of a family who regularly rented one of my grandfather's cabins, and I decided to tie an anchor to a rope and jump out of a boat we had placed near the drop-off. The idea was to see how far down we could go in the darkness toward the bottom before we would need to come up. This was quite scary to me, but that was the point of the game. On about the second turn for my friend, I became worried as he stayed down much longer than I thought he should. Finally, he burst out on the surface, sputtering and gasping for air. I asked him what happened, and he told me he had gotten tangled in the anchor rope when he had tried to surface. That was the end of that game forever.

Before the floating dock was built, there existed near that spot an old conventional dock that jutted out into the river. At low tide, it was several feet above the water. Occasionally, when a rare weather front moved in with sustained winds blowing to the east, the water at low tide would be abnormally low, to the extent that the dock would be maybe seven feet above the water. Knowing about the drop-off, but not being able to see exactly where the edge of it was in relation to the end of the dock, I made an assumption. I figured it was within diving distance of the end of the dock. If I could dive far enough off the end of it, I would pass over the shallow water and plunge into the deeper water farther out. So, I backed down the dock, got a running start, and dove as hard as I could out over the water, intending to go headfirst into the deeper water beyond. Well, not being experienced in diving from that height, my intended smooth, headfirst dive with my arms extended in perfect form didn't go as planned. I tumbled over in the air and landed with a big splash flat on my back.

When I turned over, I found that the black water was only about two feet deep where I had landed, not the deeper water I thought would be there. If I had executed the headfirst dive perfectly into the shallow water, more than likely I would have broken my neck. The fact that I had awkwardly flipped over and landed flat on my back probably saved my life, or at least saved me from a crippling injury. This was a risk that could not be properly evaluated because I could not see where the deep water began—situational awareness being one of the most critical components in a bold move like this. So, I took a risk that could have cost me my life because I was essentially diving blind.

I don't mean to imply that having taken risks in childhood made me more immune to risk-taking or that, somehow, I developed an insensitivity to risk. By being exposed to risk and living to look back on the events to contemplate the worth of those risks is important to develop a basis for evaluating the risk reward of various behaviors. I can be told a stove is hot and shouldn't be touched, but sometimes the admonition needs to be fortified in reality by the burning pain of a touch. Were you told, like so many other children, of the danger of an electric shock but still had to purposefully experience it in some way to grasp the reality of it? I risked briefly touching a live wire and experienced the pain. Eventually, as one who survived those early testing years, I began to slowly learn that some things I was told were dangerous *really were*, and I shouldn't risk trying it out to see for myself.

Decisions involving risk are not restricted to the risk of physical pain. Many risky decisions involve financial risk, risk to reputation, or legal risk. Bad decisions made in these areas are often driven by emotion rather than reason or logic. Emotion overriding logic in evaluating an action usually leads to problems. Imagine risk evaluation being like an asymmetrical energy resembling a yin-and-yang configuration—with yin being emotion and yang being logic. Sometimes the yin has more positive energy; sometimes the yang does. With more experience taking risk, the logical yang gains more energy, even though the diminished emotional yin is still present. Perhaps risks survived in youth, despite the less-than-stellar decisions made, improve the ability to better judge risk-reward propositions faced later in life.

On the other hand, surviving risky behavior through good fortune overriding bad judgment may not help in later risk-taking experiences. A history of surviving risky situations through luck encourages a tendency to underestimate risk in the future. This is not a healthy mindset. Many of the decisions I have made in my working career, as well as in my personal life, involved a large measure of risk. In the book, *Outliers*, Malcolm Gladwell describes successful musicians, athletes, and other successful people as having spent some 10,000 hours developing their particular skill. Perhaps there is a corollary in developing a greater-than-average tolerance for risk and a better ability to assess the odds of success more rationally versus failure.

As an adult, I was faced with serious decisions, such as taking on a huge amount of debt for a mortgage or taking a particular action at work that could lead to something good or getting me fired. You can likely think of similar situations and how you handled yourself. For example, if I had little experience making decisions with significant risk, I would probably face a great deal of stress involved in contemplating the pluses and minuses, or the worst-case outcomes versus the possible rewards, of such big decisions. In these hours, an inexperienced risktaker is flooded with emotions taking a front-row seat to the internal deliberations. Fear of the unknown, overwhelming bouts of anxiety, and sleepless nights at times precede the moment to make the decision: go or no go.

As an innocent child, ignorant of the awful outcomes that could come from a risky decision, I didn't agonize over possible outcomes but plowed ahead. If that happened on several occasions in my early years, with the consequences of the decisions growing over time as I aged, perhaps my psyche slowly increased its comfort with risk-taking. Somehow, my early experiences with risk manifested themselves in my ability as an adult to make consequential decisions without disproportional anxiety. So, maybe as demonstrated in *Outliers*, my increasing ability as an adult to be comfortable assessing decisions with a considerable risk component comes from the many, many hours I spent earlier in life assessing risk and making decisions as a child, even without being fully aware of their impact or importance at the time.

Willingness to go against conventional wisdom when making an important and weighty decision—going against the crowd—can be risky. History is replete with examples of people who suffered for expressing their contrary views. Some had a higher tolerance for risk and were willing to risk serious harm to their reputation, even their lives, to openly express their views. One extreme example is Galileo, who incurred the wrath of the Catholic Church for his stated belief that the Earth revolved around the Sun. You and I may never get into a situation that rough, where an entire church turns on us, but we do face choices every day that have serious, personal consequences.

Risk tolerance has a profound influence on the development of character in an individual. There is bound to come a time when you are confronted with a decision that involves taking a stand on a controversial issue. Will you choose a course you believe to be the right, morally correct decision, even though it's not popular? Or will you go with a decision that will be acceptable to the majority and not cause any pain, but will also chip away at your integrity? If you have a low tolerance for risk, you may follow the easy route. But, by doing so, did you compromise your integrity and sense of self-worth?

Learning how things work and understanding my abilities and limitations are lessons that came through observation and experimentation. The freedom and curiosity I enjoyed as a youngster led to confidence and realistic caution, traits that have served me well through the years.

~⁄ι∖~

Values and Judgement

SEEING PEOPLE AS THEY REALLY ARE

I HAVE LEARNED TO BE CAUTIOUS in making quick judgments about an individual's character or motivation because of some unconventional appearance or behavior. While it is imperative to pick up signals from someone who is intent on doing harm, it is also important to differentiate signals of impending harm from signs of unusual physical or mental manifestations that are harmless. This differentiation is recognized in awareness training for police officers so they will respond appropriately to a perceived threat. There are times when stressed persons decide to end life though "suicide by cop." This occurs during a situation contrived by a distraught person to instigate a confrontation with police, or it could be improvised on the spot during a stressful encounter with law enforcement. At the height of the confrontation, a threatening move is made by the person in question, causing police to shoot.

In a conversation with the Orlando, Florida, police chief, right after one of these instances where a person wanted to be shot, the chief was pleased to report that his officers, trained to recognize behavioral differences in these situations, held their fire and were able to take the distraught person into custody rather than misreading the situation. Seeing people for who they are in the moment, rather than jumping to conclusions based on appearance alone, is an important life lesson. It's easy to be misled by physical appearance, limited knowledge of the person, or during an isolated instance of odd behavior. This applies to ordinary, daily interactions more often than it does to life-or-death situations, as with the police example.

A friend, Kenny, a masonry contractor in business with his father, told a story to me illustrating how looks can be misleading. They were very successful in their business and had become quite wealthy. Kenny was a hands-on owner in the company and often worked with his men laying blocks and brick on a jobsite. On one of those days, he left a site dressed in coveralls, covered with mortar dust and grime, to make a deposit at his bank. As he stood in line at a teller's window, the people around him kept their distance, looking down on him with expressions of disdain—surely, he was an inferior species. He allowed himself a big grin when his turn at the window came. The teller greeted him with a lovely smile and loudly asked how he enjoyed his recent trip to Paris with his wife, Barbara.

Some of the most interesting conversations I have had were with unusual people, surprising me in depth and insight, contrary to what might have been expected from a first impression based on strange or out-of-context physical appearance or behavior. Revealing insights into others are not limited to those whose outward appearances are unusual. They can also be gleaned from engaging in conversations with those who *look* "normal" but are considered by others to be strange. The reverse is also true. Some very normal-looking and acting people can indeed be worthy of caution. In a conversation with a former boss one day, I wondered how some criminals can be so successful at not getting caught. He said, "Well, the best criminals don't go around with a tattoo on their foreheads exclaiming, 'I am a crook!'"

A sixteenth-century jester, Till Eulenspiegel, or Dylulenspegel in Low German, embodied this suspicion that some who have the appearance of respectability may not be quite so if you look deeper into their character. He traveled throughout Germany, leaving behind tales of his encounters and antics that amused and entertained the crowds. His performances really served a deeper purpose, which was to expose the real personalities of the powerful figures of his time. He didn't accept what he saw on the surface but pushed to ascertain the true nature of those he encountered. He is portrayed as wearing jester's clothing. Legend has it that he carried a mirror he would hold up to the faces of clergy or royalty, asking them to peer into it to see who they really were.

I once had an unexpected, enlightening encounter with a woman who was homeless. I was standing in a reception area adjacent to my office at a university one day when the door burst open and an agitated woman strode in, trailed by two police officers. The brief explanation by the officers was that she was using one of the academic building restrooms as a washroom, apparently not for the first time. When confronted by police officers, she demanded to see someone in charge—so they directed her to me. Curious, I told the officers they could leave her with me, and I invited her into my office for a conversation. Their faces showed their doubt in my judgment, but they decided to go along with me anyway, and they turned and left.

This impromptu visit presented an opportunity to gain insight into the life of a person living on the street, even though it was information from only one person's perspective in the way it was conveyed to me. Her way of life was very different from any of my experiences. Angela, as she introduced herself, probably in her sixties, had once been an accomplished professional and she had a college degree. In the early years of her life, a woman she knew was posted overseas on a job who asked Angela to accompany her as an assistant. The time she spent living in Europe, Angela explained, was marvelous and lasted for a span of several years. Then, I heard an intentionally vague story of some corruption that caused her friend to lose her job, which led to their return to the United States. The exact circumstances of their return were not revealed to me in a way that I thought credible, but I was there to listen, not criticize.

On her return to the United States, Angela became somewhat of a drifter, *somehow* having lost her passport and any meaningful identification papers. Again, I just listened and did not probe. As she continued her story, it became more detailed regarding her life "off the grid." She was not really living a homeless life in her mind. She seemed to enjoy each day with no responsibility and no one to answer to. However, as time wore on, she suffered accidents that began to compromise her physical abilities, and age began to take its toll. In one accident, she fell to the pavement from the steps of a public bus, bloodying her knees and causing a great deal of pain. The bus driver, no doubt discounting her worth and not wanting to be troubled with assisting a homeless person, refused to allow her back on the bus. It was nighttime, and she limped two miles alone in the dark to a hospital emergency room. She relayed this story as representative of how she was seen by others during this time in her life.

Her daily routine, at least during the time when I met her, consisted of being allowed by a local grocer to sleep at night in a covered area where shopping carts were stored. I was not clear on the details, but I think she was also offered some food items by the grocer that were past their "sell by" date. Each morning, her routine took her to another grocery store—not too far from the first—where she sat in the entry lobby, drinking their complementary coffee and reading the daily paper. Next, she went to a nearby post office where she checked her box for mail. She used public facilities to take care of her daily ablutions, like the restroom on campus that brought her to my attention.

The day I met her, she was looking pretty rough around the edges. After our initial conversation, I volunteered to put her in contact with a social services agency that could provide some temporary respite over the weekend. They had an arrangement with a local hotel for circumstances like this, allowing Angela to stay for a couple of nights without charge. When she returned to my office on Monday as we had arranged, she looked much fresher and brighter. As I came out of my office to greet her, I saw her comfortably sitting in the reception area, reading a copy of *The Wall Street Journal* that had been lying there. When I remarked on that with possibly a little surprise in my voice, she took umbrage, commenting that she could read! She was intelligent with an obvious streak of sarcasm and exuded an attitude of self-confidence, clearly a message to all that she could take care of herself—a fair warning that is needed to survive life on the street.

Added to this was a wry sense of humor that made conversations with her even more interesting, though it became obvious to me that truth was not a requirement for telling me a good story. I talked with her about her plans for the future and the potential for a job, if she was tiring of her present status. She expressed some curiosity about what I could offer. The stumbling block was the fact she possessed no documentation proving her status as a United States citizen. The jobs I was aware of required proof of citizenship. I learned, through some pro bono legal assistance, she would need to contact the United States State Department to get the necessary documentation.

As a result of gaining this information, she took the initiative, acquired the paperwork needed, and sent it to the State Department for review. A few days later, she came back to see me and proudly waved a response to her inquiry, announcing that she had what she needed for me to help her obtain a job. I asked to see the letter she was waving around, so she reluctantly handed it over. After a quick glance, I told her the letter was simply an acknowledgement of her request, not a determination of her citizenship. The look on her face told me she knew that but hoped I wouldn't check. Her years on the street had taught her a lot about manipulating strangers for her benefit. Unfortunately, for her, I understood from the beginning that manipulation was a part of her personality. After our several meetings together, her normal advantage with strangers had deteriorated, as I was no longer a stranger. I believe she sensed at that point I would be of no further use to her, so a few minutes later, she left my office and that was the last time I saw her.

About a year later, I learned from a police officer that she had suffered a stroke and collapsed in a local store. I never heard about her again. Her story was one of a bright beginning, a sudden reversal of fortune, and transitioning from a person of respect to an anonymous person on the street, eating leftovers and sleeping with shopping carts. However, she adapted to street life for years, embracing a newfound freedom from responsibility. Angela had no desire to seriously pursue leaving that life—until it inevitably began to unravel, as age and physical decline crept into the picture. This story is of a life that ultimately ended with a lonely death on the floor of a public store. The story is a sad one, from a promising life that Angela said was filled with joy and excitement while she was in Europe, to one that changed abruptly through dark circumstances intentionally not clearly revealed to me.

This mysterious turn of events led to a blooming desire afterward to avoid responsibility and choose a life of independence, forsaking material comforts, any form of safety net, and living on the street. She seemed comfortable with her choice. Spending time with her gave me an inside look at an alternate way of life that avoids responsibility to anything other than oneself. Homelessness is a horrible and sometimes deadly experience for many who would never, ever, choose such an existence but nonetheless find themselves there. Angela was not one of those. She was a complex person, very interesting, and someone who could never be fully understood by simply looking at her outward appearance and non-conventional behavior.

I learn a great deal about life, personal motivations, joy, and tragedy by listening to others' tales of personal experiences. At times, I feel like a human sponge absorbing other peoples' pain. But listening to such tales can, when I let them, help me understand and deal with some of the pain that is inevitably in everyone's life, including my own.

EARLY ENVIRONMENTS

THE HOUSE GRANDFATHER KEEFE BUILT IS worth commenting on, as I know it had an impact on my thinking about how to affect the quality and comfort of my living environment as I grew older. The structure was a wood-frame, one-story house built in the Craftsman style, which was popular in the 1930s. The wood used was cypress, a material more available for construction then, but not in later years. Cypress is very resistant to rot and insects, which is a very important feature anywhere but particularly in the South, where the cold in the winters is not often cold enough nor prolonged enough to meaningfully reduce the insect population, including termites. Add to that moisture from humidity and rain in the summer months, and the result is that wooden houses require a great deal of maintenance to last. Cypress is exceptional in resisting these problems and in lowering the maintenance required by houses that are built with more commonly used woods.

The front yard, and one side of the house, had grass, but the backyard, where most of the family's outdoor activities took place, was dirt under the shade of several very large pecan trees. Chains from the fork of one of the pecan trees suspended a two-seat wooden swing, with arms and a comfortable back, made by my grandfather. Near the swing were outdoor chairs that together formed a very nice outdoor seating, conversation, and workspace. As this was South Georgia in a time before air-conditioning, the shaded outdoor areas were the preferred spots for spending days in the humid heat of the summer.

Near the house, facing the lane that ran adjacent to the side of his property, he built a garage with materials similar to the house.

The garage had a big wooden double door, with a chain looped through holes in the center where the two doors came together. He was quite proud of the large padlock he used with the chain to secure the doors. The padlock had an exceptionally large key, and the end that he would insert into the lock was shaped like a "T." He explained to me that during the Depression, and the subsequent gas-rationing during the war, gas theft was a problem. Gas would be siphoned out of the tanks of unsecured cars at night, a problem he avoided with his special precautions; it certainly worked for him.

On the back wall of the garage, I saw his World War I helmet hanging on a nail adjacent to the gas mask kit he carried during that time. Souvenirs, I guess, with interesting placement when I think about it. It was a rough time for him during the war years, but he hung on to these memorabilia and decided to keep them in the garage rather than in the house. I know he was deeply influenced by his wartime experience and wanted to keep some physical relics of the time—but not so close as to be a daily reminder. I have some similar objects from earlier times I can't seem to part with and tend to put them in a place where I see them only when I choose to do so.

Grandfather installed an attic fan to move air through the house, and there was an open crawl space underneath the house that allowed airflow. The foundation was supported by brick piers. The windows were fairly standard for the time and double hung, which allowed for a window to be opened either at the top or at the bottom. People living in the South prior to air-conditioning developed an art in opening some windows in the house at the top and others at the bottom to maximize the airflow throughout. Adjustments would be made as to how much each window should be raised or lowered as part of the magic of getting the best airflow.

The exhaust for the attic fan was directed downward from a large-screened opening in the ceiling of the front porch. This may seem strange, exhausting the warm attic air out over a sitting area on the porch, but it made enormous sense. As the air moved several feet down from the ceiling to people sitting on the porch, it lost most of the heat but provided a very welcome air movement on those still, sultry summer days. When I was much older, I adopted a saying that "we choose the environment that controls us." There is a relationship between what I absorbed living in that house and my thoughts about my environment later.

We had a large, fenced area just beyond the backyard for chickens. There were probably eight or ten hens at any given time. My grandfather had another small outbuilding, which contained square nesting boxes against one wall, stacked about five feet high and five feet wide. The chickens sat in these to lay their eggs, which we then gathered to eat or give away, if there were too many for us. I occasionally helped with the gathering. Too short to see into the top boxes, I would stand as tall as I could, or maybe on the edge of the bottom box, to reach up into the top nest to feel for eggs. After having my hand pecked by a chicken, and then hearing stories about how sometimes snakes would get into the boxes after the eggs, I limited myself to only gathering eggs in the lower boxes where I could clearly see what was there. I enjoyed helping Grandfather scatter corn to feed the chickens and developed an affinity for a couple of favorites. That worked out well for them, as I was sometimes the one who had to determine which chicken would be chosen for the Sunday dinner.

On the far side of the chicken yard, separated by a wire fence, was a vegetable garden. Produce from the garden—squash, tomatoes, cucumbers, and beans—supplemented our meals when the vegetables were in season. Some were canned for use in other times of the year. Pear trees and pecan trees further supplemented our food supply and added another dimension to a sustainable lifestyle.

I vaguely remember standing in the yard with my dad, looking face to face with some big white turkeys he decided to raise one year. Standing there, Dad noticed the proximity of the turkeys' heads and beaks to my head on my short, little body. He told me later he realized the danger should one of the turkeys decide to take a peck at one of my bright, shiny eyes, and that was the end of his foray into raising turkeys.

The white turkey story reminds me of a white rabbit I had when I was about four. It was quite a good-looking rabbit, and, for a time, I played with it as I probably would with my stuffed teddy bear. In the warm weather, it was rare that I would wear a shirt and just wore my usual shorts and sandals. One afternoon, when I was cuddling the rabbit against my bare chest, the rabbit decided he had enough of that and clawed his way out of my grasp with powerful kicks of his back feet, aided by scrabbling with his front paws. My chest was seriously scratched and bleeding. It was the lesson that wild animals, as opposed to stuffed toy friends, should be approached and handled with respect for what they are. However, that episode didn't lessen my appreciation and fondness for wild animals. Instead, it taught me that just because we call some of them "pets," they still have their own minds that are conditioned by survival in their native habitats. They are not inclined to be subservient to our desires.

Perhaps this lesson spilled over in some fashion to later human interactions. People have characteristics like our wild brethren: each of us has our own personality, and we aren't always willing to be subservient to the desires of others. Decisions on the quality of relationships should be based on a perception of the whole of the personality. For relationships to be healthy and long-lasting, there is a requirement to accept some traits in the personalities of others that are not particularly endearing as simply part of the package. In a counterintuitive way, like the personalities of wild animals, such unpredictability may actually make the other person more interesting.

TRIBAL BOUNDARIES

WHEN I WAS SIX YEARS OLD, we moved into a house in a suburban neighborhood in Waycross, Georgia. It was a nice neighborhood when I lived there in the 1950s and early 1960s. In those days, doors to our houses were never locked. The local dry-cleaning establishment had a man who would pick up clothes from our house. When he returned them, he'd knock on the front door, open it, and lay the cleaned clothes in their wrappers on the floor by the door and leave. It did not matter if we were home or not. Milk deliveries were similar in that the milkman, always a man, would knock on the door, open it, and announce he was there. If he heard no objection, he would go into the kitchen and put the milk bottles in the refrigerator and leave. Neighborhood children would come and go between each other's houses. Cars were left parked on the side of the road in front of each person's house, unlocked. Theft was just not a problem. There was a mutual sense of trust in the neighborhood. Strangers, however, were rare and were noticed with some suspicion. Perhaps within our boundaries, our neighborhoods, we had a sense of security stemming from a mutual protectiveness inherited from our ancestral generations.

One afternoon, a friend and I observed a couple of men walking through the surrounding neighborhoods. Strangers in the tribal boundaries! We had never seen them before and, based on the dress suits they were wearing, we decided they must be spies. Okay, this was an illogical conclusion as to what stealthy spies would wear in a residential neighborhood, but we saw what we wanted to see. So, we spent what seemed to be an hour sneaking behind them, hiding in bushes, behind trees, and any hidden place to keep the spies from seeing us. Finally, we saw them knock on a door. Someone inside the home opened the door, and they went in.

It was getting dark, so we decided to run to my house and download all of our clandestine observations to my mother. When we got to the part about the spies being let into a particular house, she allowed that she knew the woman who lived there. To our delight and surprise, she telephoned the woman and asked about the men who had dropped in. To our total disappointment, Mother learned that the two men were on a sales call and pitching an encyclopedia to the homeowner. We sometimes did let our imaginations run a little too wild, but we spent our free time dreaming up creative ways to have fun. That particular game of following the strangers is an example of our conditioning to watch for outsiders in our area.

Today, in my current suburban neighborhood in Florida, walking is a pleasant means of exercise and provides an opportunity to meet neighbors who are also out in their yards or walking along as well. There is a cul-de-sac a short distance away from my house that I sometimes walk through, but not on a regular basis. A lot of young families with toddlers and grammar school-aged children live there. A neighbor told me that every week or so, they gather in one of their yards facing the street to socialize.

One Friday afternoon, I ventured around this cul-de-sac while they were gathered in a front yard, spilling out onto the sidewalk and into the edge of the street. As I walked by, I became conscious of the group's studied avoidance of eye contact with me. In one moment, the mother of a child made brief eye contact, but she quickly looked away so as not to need to acknowledge my presence. Even though my home was little more than two blocks away, I was the outsider, a person to be viewed with suspicion and not to be shown any sign of openness or welcome inside "their" territory.

There are no distinguishing differences between us, other than I am about forty years older than the oldest of them. But that shouldn't have triggered alarm. The main difference was they simply didn't appear to recall seeing me before. I was a stranger. On other days when I walk the streets I more commonly frequent, I will see individuals or couples along the way who give a friendly wave and greeting. They have seen me walking by more than once before and accept me as "belonging" there.

DISCIPLINE AND GUILT

OVER THE DECADES, THERE HAVE BEEN different views on how parents should discipline their children. Spanking, no spanking, timeouts, room confinement, grounding, and even more methods to instill discipline or punishment for real or perceived wrongdoings have been in vogue at one time or another. When I was a kid, minor offenses were simply dealt with by an oral reprimand. Any acts my parents thought deserved more would result in a "whipping," or, alternatively, getting "switched." Those words may sound harsh but where we lived, the milder term, spanking, was not used to describe what was going to happen. Such physical punishments were rarely used—there are only four or five times in my life I can remember. The method that had more psychological effect than physical pain was the preparation for getting switched; this only happened to me once.

Mother decided some action of mine deserved a switching. She ordered me to go to the yard and pick a switch and bring it back in for her to use on me. I had a choice of two bushes. One was called a beauty bush, which had long reddish-brown stems. When the leaves were pulled off, this stick made a very smooth switch that made a scary sound as I flicked it through the air. The other choice was to pick a branch from a spirea bush, which had a rougher texture on the stem when it was cleaned of its leaves. It didn't have the scary sound, but the rough bark looked ominous. Part of the psychological pain of this exercise was first deciding which switch would hurt the least: the smooth switch or the rough switch. Then, and maybe the hardest part, I had to decide how long the switch I picked should be. If I brought in one too short, I was afraid it would be rejected, and my mother would go out and pick a tree branch herself! So, I agonized over the length. *What is the smallest switch I could pick that she will accept?* This decision was infinitely more painful than the ultimate physical switching.

Another time when I was in trouble and anticipating a whipping in my immediate future, I tried to outrun my mother. It was precipitated by some incident happening while we were both standing in the kitchen. When Mother threatened me, I decided to make a run for it. I got as far as the screen door at the front of the house and just as I had almost made it to freedom, both hands out in front of me and slamming the screen door open, I felt Mother grab the back of my shirt and pull me back in. I don't recall what happened next, but I do remember being amazed at how fast Mother could run.

There is one other notable time when Mother's temper flared at something my brother Lowry and I had done together. She yelled at us to lie across her bed while she quickly reached into her closet and grabbed the closest of her belts and began hitting us. I was surprised when it began because it was like being hit with a feather. I turned my head to Lowry and we both did our best to stifle laughter, as Mother in her haste had grabbed a very light cloth belt. We failed at holding back our laughter about the same time as Mother realized what she was doing. I glanced back and saw the look of puzzlement on her face just before she too started to laugh. That ended with all three of us lying on the bed, uncontrollably laughing. For me and my brothers, physical punishment was meted out very rarely but, when it was, it was usually deserved, and it was done in a way that did not create doubt about our parents' love for us.

It was always clear the punishment was for our actions, not a statement of disapproval for who we were as persons. These early experiences of being punished and having the degree of punishment appropriate for the infraction was important in my development. Other children's experiences with physical punishment may not have been as fair as I believe mine were. In fact, I have heard stories of egregious assaults on kids by parents in the name of discipline as you have, no doubt. I was fortunate not to be one of them. I also understood my parents' clear expectation that bad behavior was unacceptable on my part. This had a positive impact on my character development. The fact that discipline was only handed out in a manner that I, even as a child, accepted as fair was a crucial part of the positive outcome. I believe this dynamic helped me in my role as a vice president at two universities where, for a total of thirty-two years, part of my responsibilities involved personnel departments reporting to me. As you can imagine, employee discipline is necessary from time to time, and good judgment is crucial for the work force to accept that the disciplinary actions are fair.

During my time in first grade in the small country school where I started my formal education, I witnessed on a regular basis the underlying value proposition that actions have consequences and learned from it. One boy in my class, Wyndell, was constantly creating problems with his behavior. The consequence was that about every two weeks, our teacher held up Wyndell by one arm in front of the class and spanked his bottom with a wooden paddle. As Wyndell screamed and cried, invariably, the girl in the seat in front of me would begin to quietly sob along with him. We learned a lot about action and consequence from Wyndell. We absorbed the concept of the use of discipline to maintain order and adherence to rules regarding unacceptable behavior.

The grades our class received on papers we had turned in were not overly secret, so our desire to get good grades was enhanced by seeing the praise given to students for good work and high marks. This was another impactful demonstration of actions and consequences. I was subjected to a version of this motivational tactic in the ninth grade, one which was rather draconian. After each test was graded and the papers were returned to the students, the teacher had us rearrange our row seating in the classroom by the order of our numerical grade on the test. When we had found our new desks, those with the highest marks sat at the front, while the teacher publicly berated the student in the last seat for getting the lowest grade.

Interestingly, a version of this ninth-grade process of "shame" motivation was practiced when I was in the military in officer candidate school. Three times during the sixth months of training, we were gathered, and each candidate was given a sheet of paper numbered one through sixty, with sixty being the number in our class at the beginning of the training. In each of these three sessions, we were required to evaluate our fellow candidates in numerical order as to how effective we believed they would be if commissioned as an officer. We had to put someone's name in the number one slot and someone's name in the number sixty slot. The other names we filled in between top and bottom had to be in the order we believed represented their place in the class. At the end of each of these rating sessions, the three candidates with the lowest scores were summarily dismissed from the program, with the time spent to date not counted against their required time in the military. It was a brutal but necessary part of our training. We were experiencing the reality of making judgments about the performance of others—something we would be required to do as military officers should we make the cut.

Being disciplined as a child, experiencing the phenomenon of cause and effect, and seeking approval of the adults around me as I grew up led to another emotion that begins to develop in childhood. That is a feeling that has been labeled "guilt." A child looks to the adults around them as role models. They desire to please them and have them react in a positive way. Once the child begins to comprehend that some actions have the opposite effect—the adult's displeasure—it does not result in a positive outcome. Interestingly, adults don't seem to do much, if anything, wrong that a kid is aware of. And they certainly don't confess to a child when they have misbehaved in some way. However, it seems as though elders are always aware of any misbehavior on the child's part. This can lead to a child thinking that they are the only one that does bad things—after all, the adults in their life don't seem to.

When a young person decides not to tell their parents something they know will displease them, that lack of disclosure itself begins to feel like a bad thing. This too contributes to the development of a sense of guilt. It's perceived as something new and unpleasant, but it's an emotion we carry the rest of our lives, especially surrounding different actions we take that we sense we shouldn't have. To complicate this situation even more is that guilt can be used as leverage over others, beginning with its use as a tool by those same adults in the child's life. Some relatives seem particularly adept at wielding this psychological tool and the older relatives are the most skilled.

Guilt has been built into the practice of many religions with great effect, so why not in family dynamics? Like many things, moderation is the key. A little sense of guilt over something we have done can prevent us from repeating a misdeed. But too much guilt can be absolutely debilitating. Guilt is a human response to thoughts or actions we have been conditioned to believe are wrong, and the relative strength of that guilt response is formed at an early age.

SELF-RELIANCE

My grandmother, Alma Keefe, told a story that included references to a small country store maybe three miles away from their home in Jamestown. The market didn't offer the variety of merchandise the grocery store did, but it had everyday staples and was a comfortable place for locals to congregate and share news and gossip. We rarely went there, but my memories are of visits in the fall or winter because I clearly recall the pleasant smell of the wood-burning stove that provided comforting warmth from the outdoor chill. Several men would be sitting around that stove on wooden chairs, some smoking pipes, talking and laughing among themselves. They dressed in clothes suitable for working farms: denim overalls, plaid flannel shirts, and heavy jackets. The other smell that permeated the large, one-room store was from the fatback bacon that was sliced up for sale. The combination of the wood smoke and the fatback bacon is indelible, one of those smells I'd recognize again immediately. Couples frequented the place, with the women mostly purchasing meat, sugar, salt, and other staples, while the men mostly hung out for the camaraderie. It was a pleasant place with a friendly atmosphere. I felt good being there.

The story my grandmother told took place before I was born, possibly in the late 1930s or early 1940s. Several of the men around the store knew my grandfather was out of town working during the week. One of them, having had a drink or two, announced to the others gathered there that he was going up the road to visit my grandmother, with an obviously amorous intent. She was young then, of course, and certainly not a "grandmother," even though in this story that's what I will call her. When the man reached the house and banged on the door, Grandmother saw who was there through a window. When she noticed the signs he'd been drinking, she quickly fetched an automatic pistol she kept for protection. The pistol, which I have today, is a .32 caliber Ortgies. She opened the door and before he could push his way in, she raised the gun and he started to run away. Quite scared, she fired a shot at him, which hit and splintered some wood off a utility pole he had just ducked behind. The pistol automatically reloads, so no further cocking is necessary for firing again.

Not being that familiar with the gun, she thought she needed to cock it and jerked back the slide. Panic had set in, so when she jerked the slide back, she pulled upward on it at the same time, which is the maneuver necessary to disassemble the weapon for cleaning. So, the pistol fell apart in her hands. She dropped to the floor crying, she said, trying to reassemble it. Turns out, it didn't matter because by this time, her frightened suitor had fled the scene. Local lore has it that when he met his buddies again, who were still smoking their pipes and warming themselves around the wood stove in the store, he warned them all to "stay away from that Keefe woman or she will shoot you!" Grandmother's reputation was made. She never had unwanted male visitors again.

Another story involves Grandfather Keefe when he was dating my grandmother, whose given name was Huggins. They didn't call it dating in those days; it was more like just calling on a girl.

Grandmother's parents died early, and she was shifted around from one family of relatives to another. Times were hard, so an extra mouth to feed was not particularly welcome. One family she was staying with had older boys who decided out of meanness that they didn't want my grandfather to see their cousin, my future grandmother. They learned he was planning to visit her at their house one Saturday night. The word circulated back to Grandfather that when he approached their house that night, they were going to "beat him" to the point he would never want to come again. Knowing that, Grandfather walked the last stretch to her house on railroad tracks that were built above the surrounding land. It was a moonlit night, according to the story, and Grandfather began to whistle as he walked to make sure her cousins, who he suspected were hiding somewhere nearby, knew he was coming.

Sure enough, they emerged from some bushes and began running up the slope to the tracks where he was walking, yelling threats. Grandfather, a World War I combat veteran, pulled a pistol from his pocket and began calmly firing into the ground all around their feet and legs. They turned tail and ran away. He said they never again threatened or bothered him as he continued to call on my future grandmother. Both grandparents were obviously not to be trifled with.

These stories of my grandparents are clues to the development of my sense of the world and how it works. They were two very capable adults in my life. They did not have easy upbringings, so they learned early on to take care of themselves and were able to carve out a good life with no outside financial help. They valued family relationships, family that extended to a multitude of in-laws and cousins who lived within a five-mile radius of their house. We had a lot of interaction with them when I was young. I don't recall too many visitors that were not family. In our family gatherings, I didn't hear them brag about accomplishments or anything they had done. They seemed to be happy in the lives they had made for themselves and comfortable with who they were. Observing them in their daily interactions—and listening to the stories they told mostly for our amusement—had a lasting impact on me. In-between the lines, I absorbed the hidden meanings of how to apply principles and make judgements in a variety of situations. Their character traits, handed down freely and without expectations, contributed to how I view life today.

-/\\\-

Reasoning and Logic

CONSEQUENCES AND COMPASSION

IN THE WINTER OF 1948, DAD found two baby rabbits in a nest by the railroad tracks across from the house we lived in with my grandparents. There was evidence of a scuffle and tufts of hair in the tall grasses near the rabbits' nesting place that led him to conclude that a predator had killed their mother. He brought the babies home and made them a nest of straw in an empty pen we had outside of the house for some other little animal we no longer had. I pleaded with him to bring them in the house out of the cold. He insisted that they were wild creatures and used to cold weather. Well, the next morning when we went out to feed them, they had died of the cold. I could tell Dad was really shocked.

What we figured out later was the baby bunnies depended on cuddling against their mother for warmth in the cold nights. I had a similar experience with a turtle I kept as a pet. I housed him in a bowl of water containing a little rock hill for him to perch on. It was wintertime, and our house was not super warm. Before I went to bed, I placed the bowl on top of the coal-fired space heater, thinking that would keep him cozy through the night. The next morning when I went to check on him, the water had evaporated, and the turtle had died from the heat. It was my turn to be shocked!

I made decisions when I was young to do something I thought was a good thing—it was the right choice to make and something I believed would make me and others happy. Then things went wrong. Something unexpected occurred that was never anticipated, resulting in shock and hurt. For children, the consequences of actions that unexpectedly go horribly wrong are valuable learning situations. No matter how honorable the intentions are when making a decision, there are times when the outcome will be an unexpected failure. Maybe this is nature's way of preparing us to deal with similar situations, some which will have much more severe consequences, when we reach adulthood. It is important to accept the fact that negative surprises will happen. The key is not to allow an unexpected failure to become overwhelming and debilitating.

My feelings of devastation with the deaths of the little rabbits left out in the cold cause me to wonder if this was the beginning of developing a sense of compassion. Then, I think about my attitude while picking which chicken would be sacrificed for our Sunday dinner. While I had my favorites and protected them, I don't recall worrying too much about the one I picked to be killed. Why the difference? I'm not sure. It may be because of my upbringing in a rural area where animals were raised, it was understood they were a part of our food supply. For the practical adults I lived with and learned from, this was simply the way life was. A strong sense of compassion for the animals raised for food could be problematic. The bunnies, however, were not part of our food supply, so I may have been conditioned to think of them differently. The childhood stories that were read to me, and that I later read myself, were filled with bunnies, baby deer, cuddly teddy bears, and colorful songbirds. Very little was written in the stories I was exposed to about the fate of farm animals raised for food. Perhaps this presented some early conditioning on disseminating compassion; was discrimination felt in the world of people as opposed to animals? Could that explain later feelings of compassion for entire groups of people as opposed to feeling little for other groups, based on stories told to me as a child? I think that is absolutely the case.

There is a proverb, "As the twig is bent, so shall grow the tree." There's some truth in that, but people are not trees. For example, I can observe, think, and adjust some of my earlier beliefs ingrained by childhood experiences and the stories I heard if I choose to do so. Choosing anything is just that; it involves a decision and a choice. First, I must be mindful enough to realize I even have a choice. To this point, I like what Winston Churchill said, "Men occasionally stumble over the truth, but most of them pick themselves up and hurry off as if nothing had happened."

There is a contradiction to what I said about having little compassion for the farm animals that are part of our food stream. When I was about twelve, my grandfather bought a steer, what he called the young cattle he raised for food, to supply his family with beef when it had matured. He had done this before, but I hadn't paid close attention to the process. This time, however, I took it upon myself to go into the field at times and play with the young steer. We would chase around, and I would grab him by the head to push him back and forth. It was great fun for both of us. Then, there was an interlude of several months between my visits with the young steer. When I returned to the field after this absence to play, my how he had grown! I believe he recognized me because he let me walk up to him and grab him by his horns. To my surprise, when I tried to shake his head to move him around as I had before, it was as if I had grabbed the front end of a truck, trying to shake it.

The steer lowered his head to charge me, in a playful way to him I'm sure, but now that he was much bigger than me by far, I immediately sensed a problem. I began to run for the gate. I had a small head start but he rapidly gained on me. The gate was a big, wooden field gate, and it was closed. When I reached it, I didn't slow down to try to open it. Instead, I jumped up, about waist high, to the top of the gate, and my forward momentum caused me to hit the gate and flip over it, landing on my back in the dirt lane on the other side. The event was all play for the steer, but it could have been extremely painful for me. There were no hard feelings but just the opposite. I became sad when the time came for the steer to be sent to the butcher shop, where the parts and pieces would be wrapped and stored in a freezer locker for the family. I couldn't bring myself to partake in any of that steer later. I think the experience led my grandfather, who knew of my attachment, to abandon the practice of raising a steer for the beef. This ordeal did not dampen my appetite for beef, however; I just don't want to know the particular animal it comes from.

During my steer encounter, I gained some insight into human relations. Before getting to know this animal, I thought of steers, or cattle, as only a general group of animals raised for food. That was what I was conditioned to think in my rural environment. However, when I began to pay attention to this one individual steer, playing with it and developing a connection, the animal was no longer only part of an amorphous herd, simply existing to provide food for humans. Instead, he was a living being I got to know and appreciate on an individual basis, much as I had developed a relationship with my dog, Riley.

Similarly, as a member of a human monoculture in my small world as a young person, I tended to think of people in stereotyped groups. I did not consider members of other groups as individuals but as being all the same and lumped into whatever ethnic or cultural group I identified them with. As I grew older, and my contacts with people outside my limited, youthful experience expanded, I began to see people as individuals and appreciate them for who they are, not as just one of a block of clones. I may be making a big jump to go from an experience with my pal, the steer, or my dog, Riley, to relations with people, but those connections had an influence on me.

My daughter Claire was with me as I was driving one afternoon in rural Virginia when she was maybe four years old. As we passed a farmer's field and she saw the cattle grazing, she broke into tears. I asked her why and she told me that looking at the cows in the field, it hit her where the meat in the hamburgers she liked so much came from. So, I saw the next generation beginning to have these realizations of conflict. A process was beginning of developing a personal reconciliation of how and what feelings to block in order to create emotional distance between the source of some activity and the result of that activity my daughter wished to participate in. This story involves feeling bad about what happens to a cow but, in a contradictory sense, enjoying eating a delicious hamburger.

These conflicting emotions can lead to purposeful disassociation, compartmentalizing aspects of feelings and beliefs that are contradictory. In some ways, this is very useful to maintaining sanity, but such distancing can have serious, societal consequences in other areas of life. This mental compartmentalization is another development along life's journey that allows me to participate in an activity I choose but separates me from a disturbing precedent to the activity. It is important I recognize this phenomenon so that I will, on some conscious level, know when I am compartmentalizing and not utilize these mental gymnastics to allow me to be guilt-free to embark on some behavior I would normally consider morally wrong. While shopping, there is joy in spotting a bargain in fashionable clothing. The joy can be sustained if I ignore the likelihood that the bargain price was made possible by the garment being made in a country that exploits its workers, including children, treating them like chattel and forcing them to work in deplorable conditions. It is important to have, at some level of consciousness, an awareness of this mental compartmentalization phenomenon, so as to not let it happen if it serves to mask an immoral course of action.

ADAPTING TO CHANGE

THE RURAL ENVIRONMENT WHERE I STARTED life was great for learning. However, while I portray that life as idyllic, and in some ways for a child it was, the way of life that nurtured me was not sustainable. The lifestyle of the earlier years in America was workable partly because of low population density not overstressing the land. In my childhood, family incomes were not huge, but operating expenses were very low. My grandparents' home had a septic field for wastewater and a well they had dug to produce potable water. That meant no monthly bill from a county or city for water and sewer services. In earlier years, they had no telephone so there was no monthly telephone bill and certainly no bills for internet or WiFi access. Their television, when that invention came on the household scene, was a one-time expenditure for the set itself because it used a rooftop antenna or rabbit ears—a type of indoor antenna that rested on top of the television set—for access to whatever channel an antenna could pick up. So, there was no monthly cable bill. Houses had minimal wiring for electricity, as there were few electric devices to power, thus making a monthly bill for electricity minimal. The houses they lived in were paid for, so there was no monthly mortgage payment. I don't recall ever hearing about insurance premiums because I don't believe much, if anything, was insured.

Lawsuits were rare, so personal liability insurance was rare, if they bothered to carry it. There was no local government or commercially operated trash pickup, so no monthly bills or tax assessments. Much of the food was homegrown and prepared at home, minimizing meal expenses. Healthcare was pretty much on a pay-as-you-go basis. Lawncare in those days consisted of using a non-motorized mower, called a reel mower, that was pushed by hand to cut grass on a lawn. Leaves were raked by hand, and weeds or tall grass was cut with what was called a swing blade weed cutter. Since that was what everyone did, there was no peer pressure to go further in attempting to "manicure" a lawn. Yards were irrigated by rain, not sprinkler systems. Occasionally, a few homeowners would water prized flowerbeds or small sections of grass with a sprinkler on a garden hose. If the grass dried out and turned brown, it was no different from the neighbors.

Since there were no public trash removal services in those days, Grandfather devised a system that was very ecologically friendly.

First, since most food we ate was prepared from scratch, there was very little in the way of packaging waste—there was no plastic or Styrofoam in those days. Food scraps were fed to the animals, and anything left over was composted for use in the garden. The few tin cans or other non-food garbage was buried in the chicken yard. My grandfather would dig a hole a couple of feet deep and about eight inches in diameter with a posthole digger. On days when we had inorganic trash, he would drop it in the hole and kick a little dirt on top of it. I don't recall for sure, but I think a hole like that would last a month before he needed to dig another. Paper trash, of which there was very little, was burned. There was simply not a lot of trash generated in those days. It was a frugal society that did not casually cast aside anything that could be reused by the family. No fast-food packaging, water bottles, plastic containers, or plastic product wrappings were to be found. These "conveniences" all came into society in later years. As a child, I observed how my grandfather managed the environment in a respectful way and, like so many other actions I witnessed, there was a practical creativity involved in accomplishing so many of his daily tasks.

As the country's population grew, this lifestyle became unsustainable. With more people crowding the rural environment and more houses adding septic fields, the ground water became polluted, causing home wells that relied on that source of water to be unsanitary. At that point, local governments stepped in and provided mandatory connection to regional sewer systems. This action created a one-time hook-up fee in many cases and certainly created a monthly bill to be paid. It was the same when municipal water services replaced use of the now-polluted wells. These expensive new regional sewer systems relied on dumping the raw sewage they collected into the nearest river. It didn't take many years for this unsanitary procedure to be recognized as unsustainable, so the construction and operation of treatment facilities to clean up the sewage ensued. That action added more cost to the operation, costs that were ultimately passed on to customers who were hooked into the system.

Increased population drove a need to pave the existing dirt roads—all at a cost. New services that were desired by homeowners added to the family budget, such as access to additional television channels beyond what a rooftop antenna could provide, electric washers and dryers, freezers, modern refrigerators, disposable diapers for babies, and a big-ticket item added to monthly electric bills, the desire for air-conditioning in homes. Gas-powered lawn mowers became available to cut grass. Gas-powered leaf blowers and lawn edgers became popular. Soon, the race was on to keep lawns immaculate, with all of the accompanying irritating noise, pollution, and expense. All in, the low-cost lifestyle of the earlier era came to a close.

The spirit of the old ways, though, lived on with me. That included the idea of entrepreneurship, the determination to deal with and overcome hardship, and adapting to an ever-changing way of life. A moral code had been instilled and stayed with me with respect to personal responsibility for the natural environment. I adjusted my life with little sense of loss, but rather a sense of adventure and confidence embarking on new ways of living.

Earth teems with life. Humans are part of that life and witnessing how my parents and grandparents sustained their lives from the land and the society around them influenced my appreciation of the interconnectedness of all life. I found there are usually logical reasons for doing things a certain way because someone ahead of me already went through a lot of trial and error to get it right. But this is a continuing loop, and every day provides opportunities for innovation and different ways to experience life. It pains me to see so many who don't understand this connectedness and its impact on the future existence of human life on the planet.

⌇

Ethics and Morals

COLORFUL CHARACTERS

CHILDREN'S FAIRYTALES, REGARDLESS OF THE CULTURE, are filled with colorful characters, larger than life, with a common attribute—they evoke emotional responses from children hearing the stories. Further, these stories usually have a moral message, such as good triumphing over evil, that are often tied to a corollary message that ordinary people can win over powerful adversaries.

Mom gave me a blackboard mounted on an easel that, when standing, was about as tall as me when I was in early grade school. The borders of the blackboard were covered with the letters of the alphabet, numbers one through ten, and an amazing variety of fairytale characters. I learned to copy the letters and numbers and I'd try to copy the drawings of the characters. Some characters were from *Winnie the Pooh*, a book that was read to me. I was infatuated with the great artwork on the pages depicting the characters in the book. I never understood or was very interested in the story, but I was fascinated by the drawings as they stimulated my imagination. I believe these experiences influenced my adult interest in drawing and in the artwork of Monet, van Gogh, Cézanne, Matisse, and many others from the Impressionist and Post-Impressionist periods.

A book I did understand and took great interest in was *Bambi*. That story influenced my continuing fascination in the life of wild animals in the forest and added to my appreciation of the wonders of nature. The original book, published in 1923 by Felix Salten, was written in German and largely meant for adult readers. Later, English-language film and book adaptations made it more suitable for children. Still, many observations about life meant for adults are perhaps subliminally absorbed by children—as I know happened to me. One passage has to do with two leaves hanging high on a tree limb in the autumn of the year. I'll not repeat the long conversation between the leaves, but instead give my greatly paraphrased interpretation in a much-abbreviated summary to get to one of the points that stuck with me, even though I didn't understand the depth of the meaning until years later.

One leaf says to the other, "Well, it's that time of the year when our leaf friends are beginning to fall from the tree." The other leaf asks the first, "Where will we go when our turn comes to fall?" The first leaf answered, "No one has ever come back up to tell us." This strikes me as a metaphor for every human question about death we attempt to answer. Great children's books have important messages about life woven into an entertaining story, sort of like the stories my grandfather told sitting around outside with the family after dark. His colorful stories, succinctly related, usually had a theme regarding good overcoming evil.

Later in life, I read serious, scholarly interpretations of the meanings behind popular childhood stories and fairytales we read. At the time of my exposure, when I was three, four, or five years old, I interpreted the meaning based on my very limited knowledge and experience. I could absorb and understand the fundamentals, such as good versus evil, or kindness over meanness. I found a note from my mother she wrote when I was a child about how I liked the story of Red Riding Hood. Recently, I looked that story up on the internet and was astounded at how many interpretations of the story there were: explanations about the meaning behind the red color of her bonnet and cape, sexual innuendos regarding her interaction with the wolf, parts of the story as metaphors for birth, and the transition to womanhood by the female protagonist. All I can say is that I didn't get any of that! I just enjoyed the story as a simple, exciting narrative of good triumphing over evil and took it all at face value. I particularly enjoyed the drawings. So, if adults want to do a deep dive into the obscure and hidden metaphors they believe they can see in children's stories, have at it. But allow kids to interpret and absorb some of the underlying messages in the stories at a level they can understand and enjoy. Don't screw it up for them with adult psychobabble.

Maybe the imagination-provoking nature of the artwork in various children's books help explain my later fascination with the incredible work of C.H. Rockey, an iconic artist who lived in Manitou Springs, Colorado. He published a book in 2014 titled *Love Songs of Middle Time*. His illustrations in this book are phenomenal. I wish I had access to those drawings when I was a child. I would have spent hours letting my imagination roam, examining the intricate detail on every page. My wife, Ksenia, and I spent time with him on visits in 2004 and greatly enjoyed talking with him about his art and his life. During that time, he was working on a book of love songs and was interested in our story, as he was with most of the couples he got to know. He had the aura of a fairytale character—a tall man with broad shoulders, flowing white beard, long white hair, and a mesmerizing personality.

His life and art were a fable. He was a true icon in his town and spent time with budding artists who dropped by his studio, encouraging them as he viewed and commented on their work so eagerly being shown to him. We were there once when a teenage artist came in to show him a small piece of 3D art he had created. Rockey took the work in his hands, turned it over appraisingly, and pronounced the work good, stating the young artist was on the right track with his work. Beaming, the artist almost floated from the studio, having received this praise from his idol.

Maybe once a year at my grandparents' house in the country, the tinkling sound of little bells would be heard coming from the direction of the road in front of our house. Looking out, a small, covered wagon pulled by several goats would come into view. The bells we heard jingling were attached to their leather harnesses to announce their arrival to potential customers along the way. Striding through the roadside grass beside the wagon was a bearded old man who was known to the neighborhood residents. He carried a pedal-operated whetstone wheel in his wagon to sharpen kitchen knives. He had small items in the wagon, with some pinned to the cloth top of the wagon, as advertisements of his wares that could supplement a household's shortage of kitchen pots, pans, tableware, or sewing supplies. He was a popular sight and enjoyed a great deal of business. I recall my mother referring to him as the "goat man" because of the goats he used to pull his wagon.

This was a living person who seemed to be a character straight out of a kid's storybook. Later in life, when I was introduced to the character Gandalf in *The Lord of the Rings* trilogy, I had a flashback of the goat man in Jamestown and later thought of Gandalf when meeting Mr. Rockey in Manitou Springs. Sometimes, reality may not be so different from the fairytale characters I enjoyed so much. Many people I've met are as fascinating and unusual as those found in fairytales, with life stories just as interesting. I don't shy away from these people; in fact, I'm drawn to their presence as iron filings are to a magnet.

Another example of a real-life person I met who could have stepped out of a storybook was a woman who lived in a house on the lane behind Grandfather Keefe's cornfield. Miss Ellie, I will call her, was introduced to me when I was about four years old. She typically wore a big, brimmed straw hat over her long, mostly gray hair. She was not very tall, and her body was somewhat bent forward. In retrospect, that bend might have simply been because I was short and she was bending down to my level to talk. Miss Ellie was missing some teeth, but I remember she still had one of her front teeth as she smiled at me. Her cotton dress hung somewhat shapelessly over her body, down to about six inches above her sturdy lace-up shoes, somewhat dusty from walking in the lane. She carried a formidably-long, sturdy stick with her when she walked, and her laugh was more of a cackle. If I were casting a movie, I would want her for my good-natured witch. I thought she was a nice person, although it was fairly well known by the locals that Miss Ellie made her livelihood selling illegal moonshine liquor she made herself. I imagined her as a friendly witch standing over a big black kettle, stirring her brew over an open fire. I believe she was one of many characters I met through life that generated my enthusiasm and enjoyment in meeting people who are quite different from those who society considers "normal."

A story my mother told me of her time as a child in the 1930s, while growing up in that same house my grandfather built, was about a recurring adventure while walking to school with one or two other little girls each day. The walk was quite long, I'm guessing about a mile and a half, down a long hill, over a bridge spanning Kettle Creek, and then back up a hill to the distant location of the school, the same one I was enrolled in decades later. At various times of the year, gypsies would camp near the bridge by the creek. Mother was told that sometimes gypsies would steal children to sell. This actually never happened, but it was a rumor all the boys and girls fervently believed. She told me when the gypsies were encamped there, to avoid capture, she and her girlfriends would begin running as fast as they could as they neared the bridge, cross it, and continue running up the hill until they were out of wind. Arriving at home, panting and exhausted, they were always thrilled that they had managed another day of going and returning from school without being snatched. It was another true-life adventure that could have been written in one of the fairytales I enjoyed.

PREJUDICE

CHILDREN'S INTERACTIONS WITH PEOPLE WHO ARE different are not always pleasant and interesting. Negative influences can also be part of the conditioning a child receives from the examples set by the adults in their lives. Segregation was the order of the day during my childhood years and, as children, we were taught by example to be prejudiced against people who didn't share our skin color, religion, or region of birth. In life, there are positive mentors and harmful ones. When I was young, I didn't know about mentors, but I definitely learned from my parents and other family adults who helped raise me. By another name, they were my mentors.

One thing I learned through the word and deed of many of the adults in the society I grew up in was prejudice. I will not use the word "racism" because that implies there are different "races" of humans. I believe we are all of one race but with differences. That is why I prefer to talk about prejudices, which are real, but I refrain from using words that reinforce the idea that there are multiple races. It was not until I was in college that I began to seriously question some of my early prejudicial beliefs. Following college, I went into the United States Army. There, I was mixed in and worked with people from all cultures, skin colors, religions, and educational backgrounds. That exposure was a further enlightenment for me, as I lived, worked, and socialized with my fellow soldiers.

Later still, having a career in three different university settings continued my separation from my early prejudicial beliefs. The university atmosphere was different in many ways from my military experience but similar in that I was around people who were different from those in my early background. There were serious scholars, research scientists, and students from around the world. I particularly enjoyed my time getting to know students from South America, Asia, Africa, and the Middle East, or, more specifically, Colombia, Brazil, Venezuela, Nigeria, Niger, Vietnam, Uzbekistan, Russia, United Arab Emirates, and Oman. Their cultures, their views of the world, and the conversations I had with them answering my many questions about life in places I had never visited were hugely educational for me.

In these intercultural interactions, I learned much about what they all had in common and what some of their differences were. The sharpest divisions in differences were between Muslims, Jews, and Christians. In the university setting, they were all friends and socialized together. Conflicts came at the leadership level of their home countries where their leaders seemed to be in a perpetual state of hostility against some other country, often using religion to galvanize their subjects in seeing others as their enemies. One Muslim woman told me that when she went home to visit, she would never admit to anyone that she had Jewish friends at the university.

Many of the commonalities that transcend national boundaries go back thousands of years to tribal existences in larger regions where there were longstanding military alliances, strong connections between tribes through intermarriage, and trade relationships that created ties. In later times, particularly after World Wars I and II, political boundaries were established by the winners of those wars, dividing lands into newly formed countries without concern for the resulting separation of overlapping cultural histories that had endured on those same lands for millennia. To say that situations in the United Arab Emirates are different from those in next-door Oman, in a national sense, is correct. But the people living in those two countries have generations of relatives split between both.

For millennia, people have made prejudicial distinctions between different human cultures for various reasons, most of which I think were originally based on survival—with a dose of greed and ego in the leadership. Over generations, those who ruled recognized that they could use the basic human survival instinct, combined with some induced fear, to convince the masses to serve them in achieving the rulers' personal ambitions. With the development of false narratives, invented threats from enemies that are different from those they rule, and with skillful messaging, they induce the population to blindly follow.

Some leaders truly care about the welfare of those they lead but, unfortunately, some leaders are completely self-serving. Part of the success of self-serving leaders is granted by a segment of the population who willingly give that power to someone who tells them what to do. This capitulation removes the need to think. They rationalize the ruler is smarter than they, so why not allow the ruler to dictate how things will be run? And, with that, people give up their freedom to make many decisions in the conduct of their personal lives.

In the very early times of our existence, humans struggled to live in a world inhabited by animals that were stronger, faster, and naturally equipped with deadly features they lacked. Humans found that they could survive, and survive well, if they banded together to face adversity. Problems started to arise later, as various bands of early humans faced scarcity in the resources needed to live. They then started to define territorial boundaries to defend and protect the resources needed for their "tribe." A culture developed in each tribe, one where outsiders could not be allowed to partake in the limited resources—game for food, arable land, and sources of usable water—in their territory. As a tribe grew in numbers, it became difficult to know and recognize on sight everyone in their tribe. How could they tell if someone belonged? Distinctions were made. Outsiders could be recognized because of their differences. Maybe it was different clothing, a different way of speaking, or maybe they didn't look like members of the tribe because of heredity characteristics, such as hair, skin, eye color, height, or weight. So, distinctions were made to identify "outsiders," and children were taught to be wary and distrustful of those outside their tribe. Prejudices soon developed.

As humanity grew in numbers and people migrated to different parts of the world, they adapted to different climates, diets, and made geographically limited selections of partners for procreation. Differences in physical appearance became apparent and minor changes in basic, physiological functioning were made to survive in different environments during hundreds of thousands of years of migration across the globe. The earlier distinctions between different tribes became more apparent and strengthened the prejudices learned from ancestors. As the world population continued to grow, shrinking geographical separations between the earlier groups became less of a barrier for intermingling. Travel became easier and faster with the use of animals, such as horses and camels, and eventually travel by sea, rail, and air made geographical isolation almost extinct. All of this led to more contact between humans who had developed different biological traits due to thousands of years of separation. The inevitable intermarriage between individuals in the different groups, or tribes, resulted in a blending of various physiological and cultural differences between groups in the population worldwide.

The social construct of distinctly different "races" among humans is fading. It seems that from one came many and now many are becoming one. This change is not happening at the same pace across the world. Nor is it happening in each country at an even pace. There are those who see this blending in society as a dire threat to their well-being in many forms; life as they know it is changing, national cultural identities are being diluted or disappearing, and there is anxiety as to whether these changes will lead to job losses or other degradation of economic security. Political leaders who benefit from the status quo and want to keep it that way tap into these fears. Laws that were changed decades ago permitting interracial marriage are being discussed in some quarters as possibly not being settled law. Some state governments are challenging the curriculum in public schools, forbidding topics to be discussed that honestly review our country's history of slavery and its long-term effects on our society. Organized religions play a big part in the existence of prejudice. When I say this, I'm not attacking religions *per se*, but I am being critical of people in positions of power in the various religions using that power to interpret the religious doctrines in ways that serve their personal beliefs as to what should be, rather than what actually is, intended in the religious texts and teachings.

Henry the VIII created an entirely new church, the Church of England, to get away from the Pope and the Catholic condemnation of divorce. He wanted religious cover for a divorce he wished to have. Fear of imprisonment or execution convinced his subjects to go along with becoming members of the new church, abandoning the old. How many crusades were fought between Christians and Muslims for control of the Middle East, Jerusalem in particular? How many of those bloody battles benefited the average person, as opposed to those in positions of power on both sides? There were times when different religions coexisted in the region peacefully. But that didn't last. After a time, one always wanted to dominate. These examples show how religion has been used as a tool to foster prejudices, prejudices that served a purpose for a ruler or a ruling class. If people the rulers wanted to control weren't Christian, or they weren't Muslim, or in other times and geographies they were not true believers in a particular faith, false narratives created myths that it was simply the fate of these non-believers to be enslaved. These unfortunates were then used to build pyramids, till fields, or provide whatever other labor was required to enable the dreams of those in power.

In recent times, relative to the long human history, early arrivals in the new world—both North and South America—envisioned the possibility of obtaining untold riches in these new lands. Just look at the name applied to the island of Puerto Rico to get a sense of the expectations. Translated into English, it means "gateway to riches." However, to truly unlock the riches, the leaders of the time determined that inexpensive labor was needed to maximize those riches. The way they saw to accomplish this was slave labor. A strong narrative justifying the practice of enslaving entire peoples includes the concept of different races, in some hierarchical stratification, superior at the top, and increasingly inferior as the "races" descended in the social hierarchy. Those at the bottom in the narrative were not considered legitimate humans and, therefore, were available for subjugation by those at the top. This fiction allowed those at the top to enslave those at the bottom without feeling guilt or any sense they were violating any of their religious beliefs.

Justifying this subjugation of people other than themselves was rationalized, as it had been for centuries, by doing it to people who were "different." The rationalization was refined by declaring that the people to be subjugated were not really humans, as were the members of the conquering class. So, it followed, in this line of selfish thinking, that it was not really "inhumane" to enslave them. After all, they were a subordinate species, or *a different race*.

Why are so many in the United States fearful of having open discussions about parts of our heritage that were horrible, such as slavery or the subjugation of indigenous populations? Why should kids believe everything in American history was noble? I think this is a great country and I wouldn't choose to live anyplace else but, as with other aspects of my life, why shouldn't I examine what bad things happened, learn from those mistakes, and use this knowledge to avoid repeating the same? Such an approach just seems healthy to me. For example, there are Holocaust museums across the country. There are constant reminders about not forgetting the atrocities committed under the Nazi regime, along with a need to understand the root causes that led to this tragic time in history, as a way to prevent these horrors from recurring in the future. But why do so many not want to talk about the history of slavery in this country and its causes and effects, so we can learn and progress? I believe these conversations should take place. People referred to as Holocaust deniers espouse the belief that the Holocaust never happened, that this event was all a hoax, despite overwhelming evidence to the contrary. I can't help but wonder if there will be a faction of the population who will one day claim that the institution of slavery in the United States never really happened, or that it was some benign movement of workers from other countries to this one.

One of my brothers told me that a relative researching our ancestry records found that some of my ancestors owned slaves in the time preceding the American Civil War. If that is true, I didn't know these people. To me, if they existed, they were no different than other slave owners of their time. I, obviously, did not live in the world they lived in all those years ago. While the thought of owning slaves today is repulsive to me, I don't know how I would have felt, or what I would have believed, at that time. It would be groundless speculation. I can say what I think and believe now, the time I live in.

When I grew up in a small South Georgia town, illegal drugs were not around. They were not available to my peers or me, so I never indulged in smoking, injecting, or swallowing mind-altering drugs. If they had been available, I would more than likely have tried them out. So, if everyone I know owns slaves, would I? I like to think not, but I don't know for sure because it's impossible to put myself in those times and circumstances. As far as I know, my ancestry is mixed, with most of my relatives coming from European countries. But my knowledge does not go back more than about four generations. That limited timeframe allows for the possibility that some of my ancestors far before then may have been enslaved. Maybe they were enslaved by Romans as they expanded their empire. However, this possibility does not alter my belief that discussions of the causes and lasting effects of that despicable practice should take place as should conversations about the Holocaust. Hearing this bit of possible family history does not cause me to feel any loss of self-worth or guilt, since I do not hold myself accountable for actions of ancestors I never knew. Nor do I feel any resentment against anyone from the distant past who might have enslaved some of my ancestors. These particular people haven't been around for generations—they are long dead. I am not *by any means* condoning the institution of slavery. I'm only saying I don't know how I would have behaved during those times.

Much of what is believed and understood to be normal is influenced by the circumstances in a person's early environment—especially by the people who impart their views to the children in that environment. A child is like a *tabula rasa*, or "blank slate," and the first impressions on the slate are embedded by the culture of the people and the society around them. It takes years of experience for the childlike acceptance of what is believed to be the normal way of the world to be challenged. I am saying this based on my own experiences. It has taken a long time for me to sculpt my own view of the world—using the material from my early conditioning, adding to it years of life experiences, and then making a conscious effort to reshape my view of what I think it all means—in order to develop my philosophy of life.

I don't doubt the argument that there is systemic "racism" in America. There is also systemic prejudice against many other aspects of humanity in America as well. I could destroy myself with guilt, anger, or an obsession with being compensated for actions of a society that preceded me if I allow my emotions to rule. That does not mean I shouldn't rationally examine that history, acknowledge it, and learn from it, with the goal of improving my treatment and respect for others. The same ancestors who included both oppressors and the oppressed built a great country. I don't think it's wise to overlook the accomplishments in our history as I examine the faults. Humans are fallible. Humans make mistakes, exercise bad judgment, sometimes despicably bad judgment, and choose lifestyles that are harmful to themselves and others. But at the same time, humans have also made enormous gains in some parts of the world, advancing civilized societies despite those shortcomings. There is not a uniform advancement across the globe, to be sure, as humans have a tumultuous history of violence and awful behaviors mixed with champions of the rule of law and social justice. That mix ebbs and flows, but it remains with us as the conflicts continue.

Arguments that discuss the topic of slavery, including its follow-on effects on lives today, could be hurtful or cause young people to "hate our country" and, therefore, shouldn't be condoned are wrong-headed. As in any worthwhile analysis of any subject, the good and the bad in society should be weighed together, without emotional distortions. The goal of the analysis and the discussions should be focused on the future, learning from the past to make the future for everyone. I believe these discussions are needed now as much as ever. Such discussions need to be infused with as much rational thought as we can summon, suppressing, as much as possible, emotional inputs fueled by conspiracy theories and age-old prejudices that are no longer serving a goal of survival but are instead now working against that goal.

History is replete with examples of atrocious behaviors committed throughout human history. Slavery is one of those despicable behaviors. The participants in instituting slavery across the world came from all cultures; cultures usually associated with skin color in popular discourse—but condemnation of this practice of slavery shouldn't be solely borne by people of one skin color, as participants in human trafficking have been historically diverse. It is a condition afflicting the one human race. An estimate of the number of the world's population currently enslaved is 40 million, according to a 2019 article titled, "One in 200 people is a slave. Why?" by Kate Hodal and published by *The Guardian*. Shouldn't there be factual, candid discussions about this phenomenon and how it affects our country's policies and us as individuals? If young people absorb their view of the world from their environment, shouldn't this environment include discussions of reality, not only whitewashed versions of reality? They won't wither and die like fragile flowers.

Based on my university experience as a student and having worked in a university environment for forty-four years, I've heard and participated in countless discussions on all sorts of topics. The discussions ranged from pleasant and cordial to heated, angry, and accusatory. These encounters broadened my perspectives, challenged my views that were not sound, reinforced those that were and, as a result, I grew as a human being. I don't want to deny young people today the opportunity to grow by participating in challenging discourse because it might hurt their feelings or because it might damage their sense of self-worth. Getting your feelings hurt and having your sense of self-worth challenged is not, in itself, a bad thing. This will happen more than once in life, so why not learn to deal with it at an early age? This is not to discount in any way the importance of self-affirming activities that are a counterweight to the negative challenges faced as one grows as a human. Both are needed.

Keep in mind that at an early age, people *hear* whatever is spoken to them. But they *don't absorb* what can't be understood through lack of experience, lack of context, or not understanding the meaning of some of the words that are spoken. Understanding, context, and life experiences come at different ages, depending on an almost infinite number of variables. That means that some topics that are important to discuss are simply not feasible for some five-year-olds, but they may be with others. These discussions can come later when each is ready. When they are ready and how much they can reasonably absorb varies from child to child.

In the 1960s, I was perusing the stacks in a college library and came across some old sociology journals from 1930s America. One of the articles I read was a serious academic debate chronicled by White writers as to whether Black people had souls, of course, assuming all White people did. I'm confident that this self-serving debate about the existence of souls was a way to justify the social order that existed at the time the article was written, as well as a rationalization of the not-to-distant history of abhorrent behaviors practiced in an economy that thrived on slave labor. This article, written a little more than half a century after the Civil War, illustrates the persistence of prejudicial thinking in a society *even after* something as consequential as the nation's bloody Civil War—during which hundreds of thousands of lives were lost—and the adoption of the Thirteenth Amendment in 1865 that officially abolished slavery. The writers may have been born in a time and place where certain prejudices were accepted, nay, required by the society they were part of, prejudices learned from ancestors that for hundreds of years preceded them. I can't get into their minds, but I suspect their views of the world and their places in it was conditioned by the influences in their childhood years, which would have been around the early 1900s, if they were writing the article published in the 1930s.

My mother-in-law, Eva, recounted an event occurring in 1925, when she lived with her parents in a small village in Pennsylvania. The Ku Klux Klan appeared in their white robes one night and burned a cross on a hill overlooking her family's house. The village was made up of recent immigrants from Europe, particularly Ukrainians. Being five years old, she was terrified at the sight. She learned later that it was a show of force to strike fear in the immigrant newcomers concerning a vote that was to be taken on some local political issue, and the adults in her village were being warned to stay away from participation. During this time in the United States, this type of event was not all that unusual. There were also stories told by the adult generation of that time that offered positive reinforcement for the activities of the Klan.

One of my relatives told me of a Klan practice in rural South Carolina around 1910. Where he lived, there was little enforcement of the law, so men of the area often took it upon themselves to render justice as they perceived it. If it became known in the village that a particular man was physically abusing his wife, the Klan would visit him one night, fully dressed in their white robes with headgear covering their faces to hide their identity. The man would be called out of his house into the darkness, lit only by the horseback men's flaming torches. The Klan leader would warn the man that word of any further abuse to his wife would result in another visit with serious consequences. If later word passed around the community that the man had again abused his wife, the Klan would return in the night, drag the man from his house, and unmercifully whip him to within an inch of his life. Stories like this were used to justify to the general population the need for the Klan and its continuing existence. The relative who told me this story passed away many years ago. I am left to simply wonder if he was a part of the group he was informing me about with such detail.

Society is responsible for determining how social order will be maintained. Punishment should not be left to vigilante justice, meted out through emotional furor with no factual basis, destroying lives unjustly. Currently, in this country, people are governed by the rule of law. But this favorable state should not be taken for granted. It is the result of a democratically elected leadership, backed by a sound Constitution as its base. If citizens ever allow this system to be weakened or corrupted by unscrupulous, self-serving elected leaders, there is risk that society will go back in time to a place where justice is determined by emotional mob behavior.

I have talked about the Ku Klux Klan in a way that may be misleading in the sense that their doctrine is relegated to history. That would be a mistake. Today, it's easy to see some of the same negative behaviors, without *any* qualities that could be called redeeming, in hate groups around the country. They fall into a spectrum of movements and call themselves by various names. They are essentially political extremists who have a view of America that is what they think it was and could become again. Their dream is not based on the reality of what was or is, simply a selfish idea of what would benefit them the most. That dream is also misguided in the sense that they believe that dream can be achieved through anarchy, a state that would ultimately harm them as well as everyone else.

From time to time in history, enlightened souls who are the first to challenge harmful prejudices being practiced against other human beings have been severely sanctioned for daring to upend the status quo. By severely, I mean shunned, hanged, burned, or imprisoned. In many parts of the world, this way of treating people who criticize a generally accepted way of life has not changed at all. In some countries, this sentiment is changing but without the buy-in by large segments of the population. Long-standing prejudices die hard and are passed on from generation to generation. Ignorance is defined as lack of knowledge or information. If children are only exposed to other humans who are like those who raise them, there is no knowledge that differences exist. What an innocent child sees is assumed to be the natural order of things. They have no sense that the views they have picked up from the adults around them are prejudiced ones. Without some intervention, these inherited prejudices will continue their march through history.

A child is a part of society, and that society's beliefs are absorbed by the child and become part of what they are, at least until a time later in life when the implications of some of the more ominous beliefs can be understood. Then comes the choice. This dovetails with the words Churchill said that I mentioned earlier, "Men occasionally stumble over the truth, but most of them pick themselves up and hurry off as if nothing had happened." When children stumble over the reality of some of their inherited beliefs, do they move on with life, ignoring it? Or do they consider revising their beliefs and the way they treat and think of others as a result? Even though these prejudices are not something a child comprehends, they are conscious of the environment they live in. They don't think about things they have never been exposed to. Unfortunately, this leaves a gaping void in the development of character. This void is filled when the child grows older. It will be filled with continued ignorance, misinformation, and conspiracy theories, or with hard truths.

There are episodes in my life that illustrate how social conditioning affected how I interacted with others and how I didn't understand the dynamics of those interactions until years later, when I could see them more clearly from the distance of time. In my first few years as a child, my exposure to people who didn't look like me was extremely limited. That slowly changed as my family moved from the rural setting to the suburbs of a small town. With four boys to care for, my mother hired a woman to come in a few days of the week to help with household chores. The Black woman she hired we called Vickie. This became my first continuing contact with a person of color. We got along well, I thought. I say, "I thought," because, at the time, segregation was in full force in the South. Many Black people held the resentment of this social circumstance below the surface during the time of my life I am talking about now. There was a surface congeniality; Vickie was an extremely hard worker but, as I look back on it, there were no conversations that I can recall that were of a personal nature at all. Such interaction was something of an unspoken taboo. As the 1950s rolled into the 1960s, the resentments surrounding segregation broke through the surface with a vengeance. Vickie became more withdrawn on what little personal basis existed, and then she worked for us no more. I don't recall the catalyst that caused the break, but I think the growing rift between Blacks and Whites was the reason. It was a time of transition.

One day, when I was sixteen and had a new license to drive, my mother asked me to take Vickie home at the end of her workday at our house. I got in the family car in the garage and, still being part of the culture of the time, I locked the passenger side front door to try, not so subtlety, to suggest she sit in the back seat. When Vickie came into the garage and grasped the front door handle and found it locked, the message was clear to her. She was being treated as an inferior person. I was not giving her the respect she deserved as a fellow human but was treating her just as all White people of the time were. She then started jerking the locked handle in a rage. I quickly unlocked it, and she got in and sat, quiet but fuming. She was in her fifties at the time and, being of an older generation than me, had years of a building anger about the treatment of Blacks by Whites.

We drove to her house without speaking, and I let her out. I remember feeling uncomfortable that some of my contemporaries may have seen me riding around with a Black woman in the front seat with me. The peer pressure to play my role in the awful dance of segregation was strong. I was conflicted. I had spent time with Vickie for years, so I felt bad about trying to force her to sit in the back seat, which was an action my social training called for. At the same time, I felt very guilty about my action. This was a period of slow transition from centuries of attitudes developed in the slaveholding years that were not switched off just because those days were declared legally over.

During the years when I was fifteen and sixteen, I spent some Saturdays when school was in session and one summer working for my dad in his lumber and building materials business. Mostly, I was a basic laborer in the lumberyard, working with the all-Black crew of men. At the time, I didn't consciously think about why I got along so well with the crew, unlike the uncomfortable feeling I had with Vickie in the car episode. These men were mostly of the same generation as Vickie. But unlike with Vickie, we had many personal conversations. I don't recall anyone holding back on what was said. I rode side by side in the cab of the big lumber delivery trucks with them. Usually, they drove but sometimes they let me drive. One man was like a relative to me and others exchanged jokes, teased, and related emotional experiences with me as though I was just another member of the group.

When the army was vetting me for Officer Candidate School several years later, I learned that the vetting included interviews with my Black co workers in the lumberyard. It went well. I think my prejudices were starting to dissolve but in an uneven way between the women and the men of the time. I never, in those years, spent any time reflecting on that difference. Now, looking back, the society I was raised in viewed interracial (as it was called) marriage to be an absolute, unconditional taboo. Any public display that suggested a personal relationship developing between a White man and a Black woman would have led to social condemnation. Working relationships were okay but any suggestion that crossing the line between that and a personal relationship was not okay. Part of my conditioning in handling these interpersonal contacts came from observing my dad's relationship with the Black men who worked for him. He had a lot of respect for them and one man, in particular, he treated almost as a brother. I say almost—remember this was the South in the 1950s and 1960s. But his attitude toward Vickie was always cool and reserved, sometimes bordering on rude. The younger members of the family definitely—and thoughtlessly—absorbed the adult behaviors and acted accordingly.

Another interaction that I didn't understand when it happened was between Vickie and my youngest brother, Jeffrey. Mother made brownies for us periodically and, on one of those days, Jeffrey was carrying his share in some sort of container. Vickie asked him to give her one. He was about four at the time and sharing was not his best attribute, so he refused. She then became demanding, and he ran out of the house to get away from her. Not to be foiled, she chased him outside and picked up a hatchet that had been left on the back porch. She chased him all the way around the house, brandishing the hatchet and demanding a brownie. He managed to beat her to the back door, entered, and sought out our mother for refuge. That was the end of the chase, and no more was said about it. We never knew how serious Vickie might have been, and nothing like that ever happened again. This was likely just another adventure for kids, but I strongly believe that Vickie was reacting to her completely understandable sensitivity to what she perceived as an insult to her as a Black person instead of simply the selfish reaction of a four-year-old, who would have refused to share with any of us. In looking back on the incident, it was a momentary crack in her façade. It must have taken a great deal of daily control to keep her stoicism in place, hiding her anger at the smothering blanket of oppression she must have felt her entire life.

I am frankly surprised and saddened to understand from my own experience how easy it is to fall into a pattern of life that normalizes hateful and disgusting behavior. Breaking free from that thoughtless and hurtful way of thinking certainly changed my worldview. It made me wonder how do these early-in-life normalizations of bad things begin? Sometimes, there is simply a child's misinterpretation of what is heard due to not understanding key words used in explaining complex thoughts. Other times, explanations of how the world works are told to a child by people intentionally omitting critical facts in the context of their explanations, leading to false impressions of reality. Without benefit of relevant worldly experience, the child naively takes the information given at face value. As experience is gained over time and the child matures, these early impressions can be challenged and changed.

When you are four years old, you interpret what you are told in the context of the limited understanding you have of the words that are used. For example, I asked my mom once why a lady in our neighborhood didn't have any kids. She told me that "nice women don't have kids if they are not married." Well, I didn't know anything about sex, barely understood the concept of marriage, but I did understand what "nice" meant. I spent a lot of time after that trying to make the connection between nice and having kids. I couldn't figure it out. There are times in adult life when we are told things that we don't understand because our life experiences haven't given us the context to comprehend the intended meaning of the message. This can lead to all sorts of misunderstandings. Think of the turmoil created in the world over misunderstandings. As a young person, I didn't face many consequences but, looking back on those instances as I grew older, the advice I can share is that when you don't fully understand something you are being told, perhaps you should try to figure it out before reacting.

As an example of views of life formed from versions of history that are selectively told, consider my childlike view of the Civil War in the United States. When I, a White youngster, was told that the Civil War was fought over states' rights and that the federal government, located in the North, was taking away the right of states to govern themselves, that is all I knew. What I was told was true, but this narrative left out the salient point that the rights being taken away from states was *the right to own slaves*. As a five-year-old who couldn't understand the concept of states' rights, and without ever hearing the slavery part, a different view of the Civil War was created. The narrative had the effect of demonizing the mysterious "North," that had forcibly taken away certain nebulous "rights" from the South. That ignorance made it easy to drift into feeling good while singing "Dixie" at high school football games and seeing the Confederate flag proudly flown. In school, I knew the words to "Dixie," but it was years before I understood the darker, underlying meaning to the line "old times there are not forgotten." As a White kid during segregation, a Black kid of my same age was rarely seen and certainly never played with. So, it was not until later in life that the inhuman atrocity of slavery came into focus for me as the major catalyst for the war. Prior to that, my early formative years were set in the monoculture society created by the adults surrounding me. Subjects that were never spoken about had an equal impact on my understanding of the universe as subjects that were spoken of.

After high school, I went to a junior college for two years. It was an all-White school in a small, South Georgia town that was predominately White. The pompous sociology professor I mentioned previously, Major Grant, reminded my class that "birds of a feather flock together," as an explanation that divisions in society along skin color lines were a natural phenomenon and needn't be questioned. This was stated without further comment and no class discussion of his observation ensued.

The day President Kennedy was assassinated, my classmates and I were in our respective dorm rooms, changing into our shorts and T-shirts for a gym class, when the announcement of the President's death came over the radio. Guys started sticking their heads into the hallway, asking in somber tones, "Did you hear what just happened?" As we walked from the dorm together, continuing our shocked discussion about what had happened, we reached the playing field where our P.E. teacher was standing. We looked at him and asked if he was aware of the President's death. He looked at us very sternly and said, "Best thing that ever happened to this country." That left us all in stunned silence. I know I had my own feelings about the event, and they were totally opposite of his. I think the other students who heard him went off to sort through their own feelings. This was a time when I began to further distance myself from some of my earlier inherited prejudices. You can learn from bad mentors. You can be faced with ugliness and that can become a catalyst for you to choose to go in another direction in life. That certainly happened to me.

Following the junior college experience, I went to Georgia State College (now Georgia State University) in Atlanta. During my time there, Dr. Martin Luther King, Jr. was assassinated, and the funeral arrangements involved a long procession walking through downtown Atlanta. The day of the procession was April 9, 1968. I was on the rooftop of a state building across the street from the Georgia State Capitol in Atlanta. Thousands of mourners in Dr. King's funeral march were just coming around a street corner into sight. At that moment, a state trooper assigned as a sniper on the rooftop turned to me and ordered me off the roof.

In that year, 1968, I was taking classes at night and working full time during the day for the Georgia Highway Department. The state building where I worked had been evacuated for the day of the funeral procession. Since I had worked my way into a supervisory role, I managed to use my limited authority, mostly imagined, to lag behind and work my way up to the rooftop to see the march from there. When I arrived, I saw an excited, young state trooper already there, positioned at the edge of a low parapet wall overlooking the street fronting the state capitol building. I could see similarly placed snipers (or as they are more benignly referred to now, "overwatch" officers) on the other rooftops facing the capitol.

When I asked him what was going on, he told me he had come in the night before from Cedartown, Georgia, as had many other troopers from posts near Atlanta, and assembled in the nearby stadium. They had deployed that morning to positions all around the capitol. Intelligence from people in the march, he told me, revealed that the crowd might attempt to storm the capitol when the procession of thousands reached that point. This was faulty intelligence as it turned out, but he wasn't aware of it at the time.

He had a high-powered rifle with a scope that he was sighting through toward the crowd coming around the corner. He had another lever-action rifle leaning against the parapet wall, along with several boxes of ammunition. He further told me (which he shouldn't have but he was obviously experiencing an adrenaline rush and being very talkative), that there were fifty officers armed with shotguns inside the capitol building, in addition to a force outside the building equipped with shields, batons, and other weaponry. He said if they tried to storm the building, "we will stack them like cordwood as high as the gold dome." At that point, he regained his wits and asked me what the hell I was doing up there on the roof. I mumbled something about being a supervisor, which he rightfully totally ignored and ordered me off the roof in no uncertain terms. So, I left.

This experience was further exposure to the stark differences in our society in tolerating—much less respecting—the beliefs and cultures of people who are "different" from them. I have no qualms with the desire to protect the state capitol building. Reflecting on the events of that day, what disturbs me now was the apparent lack of concern for the lives of the people in the funeral procession. It was if those people were enemy combatants and firing into the crowd with deadly effect would be considered a justifiable act. As time passed, and I thought about this and other events that displayed the regrettable results of ignorance and fear, I became more interested in their causes and used any influence I had in my relationships with others to educate and counteract ugly reactions to differences.

Prejudice is manifested in many ways other than skin color. People make mistakes in their lives that result in them being the object of prejudice from that time forward. For example, some mistakes involve actions that break the law and result in incarceration, fines, or other penalties that create a permanent record that follows a person the rest of their life. These misdeeds run the gamut from petty theft or a drug possession to rape and murder—each with very different degrees of wrongdoing. However, the record of these offenses is grouped into a generalized question on employment applications of, "Have you been convicted of a crime?" This leads to a hiring official being prejudiced against applicants who have answered yes to the question, without knowing the specifics of the crime or considering the potential relationship between the job requirements and the particular crime that led to the "yes" answer.

I had an encounter with this phenomenon that led to some meaningful changes at a university I worked for. I was in a public meeting with an activist group pushing for divestment of any fossil fuel holdings in the portfolio of the university. Since it was a public meeting, anyone could attend. Knowing that one of my responsibilities was oversight of the university's personnel department, one of the participants went off on a tangent regarding the discrimination she felt in the hiring process for people with a criminal history who had served their sentences and were trying to rebuild their lives. Because this topic didn't relate to the reason for the meeting, I asked her to meet with me later to discuss her concerns.

When we met, I learned that Ellen, I will call her, had spent years in prison for her role as a driver in an armed robbery that resulted in one of her accomplices, to her surprise and dismay, shooting a store clerk. As the robbery unfolded, she heard gunshots coming from inside the store followed by the shooter running from the store, jumping into the car, and screaming at her to drive. Shocked and crying as she sped away, Ellen saw a questioning look in the eyes of her accomplice. She realized he was contemplating whether he could trust her to not turn on him as a witness to what he had done. She knew at that moment he was thinking about killing her to keep her quiet. Fortunately, that moment passed and shortly thereafter, they were apprehended and went to trial, where she did testify to what she knew happened.

She sincerely regretted that major mistake in her life and was forever sad about the fourteen years she spent in prison, missing her only daughter's growing-up years. Her goal after being released was to get a decent job while working toward a college degree. Ellen quickly found that job applications required reporting any criminal convictions. That requirement led to her being screened out of contention by hiring officials before being given the chance for an interview. I understood that problem and worked with our personnel department to change the application forms to no longer require divulging a criminal history on the application until the hiring official had completed the process of selecting the final pool of candidates. Then, a background check was required for all finalists where any criminal history would be revealed. The result was that a person who had committed a crime and had paid the price required by the judicial system would at least have the chance to show their worth to a hiring official without being subjected to discrimination in the competition for an interview. Once the background check was complete and the history made known, the hiring official could then consider the whole candidate package and decide if the particulars of the criminal record made a difference in choosing who to hire for a specific job. If the job posted was for a financial position at the company, a person with a record of embezzlement would probably be out of the running at that point. On the other hand, a record revealing conviction for marijuana possession twenty years in the past would probably not disqualify an applicant for a position as an electrician.

PEOPLE AND PLACE

ONE DAY, AS A CHILD, I was inside the country house of my grandparents. It was a warm spring day, so all the windows were open. I heard someone call Grandfather Keefe from the lane running along one edge of his property. I went to the side door with him to see what it was about. He told me to stay inside while he went out to meet two men standing there. As I watched, I couldn't clearly hear what was being said but it was an animated conversation—arms waving and fingers pointing toward town. After a few minutes, the two men turned and left. When Grandfather came back to the house, looking very stern, I asked him what it was all about. He said that one of the men had a falling out of some kind with the town sheriff, and the two of them were going into town to shoot him. They wanted my grandfather to accompany them. He said he explained how bad that idea was, calmed them down, and talked them into going back home. I was impressed by how these men, determined to do harm, sought him out and listened to his advice to stand down.

In retrospect, years later when I learned more about the strength of character in my grandfather, I believe the reason they called to him that day from the lane was not so much for him to join them as they stated but because they respected him, they wanted to tell him their plan and receive the benefit of his wisdom for what they were about to do. They listened and a tragic situation for all concerned was averted. Though I did not realize it at the time, his actions that day had a lasting impact on my development. I began to be conscious of a moral obligation to intervene in troublesome situations through words or actions to head off potential harm to others. At times, this put me at risk. Sometimes I failed but sometimes I succeeded. Those successes were worth taking the personal risks and more than compensated for any efforts that failed.

In those early years growing up at my grandfather's house, my father was working twelve-hour days, Monday through Friday, and half days on Saturday. My immediate male role model was my grandfather who, at the time, would have been about sixty years old. What I absorbed, but this certainly didn't register at the time, was that it was normal for the dad of the family to work, and work hard, for the family. In those days, in the part of the country I was growing up in, the norm was for the man of the family to have work outside of the home and provide the financial resources. The woman of the family took care of the kids and everything on the home front, with the notable exception of schoolteachers, nurses, secretaries, and telephone operators. Other than those traditionally female positions, having both parents working outside of the home came later. There was a time during World War II when women were recruited into the workforce to replace the men who were called away for military service. That shift had a permanent change in the makeup of the workforce, but traditional roles slipped back into vogue somewhat as the war ended. For me, in the environment I was raised in, I saw the more traditional role as the norm. I see now that this example was setting the stage for my work ethic in the sense that my financial security as I got older was going to fall on me alone.

This belief added to my view of life that, like a baby bird jumping from the nest, when I left home at some point in my future, there would be no thought of going back. This did not bother me at all—in my view, it was just the way the world worked. My sense of independence was reinforced when I was in my twenties and planned to buy my first house. I went to Dad and asked if he would co-sign the loan with me. I wasn't asking for any money. He simply said "no." There was no explanation or excuses, just a flat no. I was able to get the loan I needed without his help, but it was a stark reminder that my financial future was up to me to work out. In retrospect, I understand his position even though he didn't explain it. He was building his own business at the time, and my mortgage obligation would not have helped his credit situation while he was maxed out buying the prior owner's company stock.

My sense of being the sole breadwinner served me well for years. But when I married Ksenia, my life changed, as she is an equal in providing financial security for us. Her story of growing up with a father who encouraged her education, career development, and financial independence had a similar effect as mine on her expectation of responsibilities and obligations. In our stories, Ksenia and I are examples of how children develop expectations of their future responsibilities and obligations by observing and living with adults. Those expectations link closely with the character of the role models who surround you in your early years. This correlation is not a given, however. As I mentioned earlier, you can have good and bad mentors in life. I also mentioned our parents are perhaps the most important mentors to us. You can model yourself after the good mentors and learn what not to do from the bad ones. However, what you consciously or subconsciously choose to do is not always consistent. You can apply your own judgment to what you see in those mentors to choose your unique path.

In my case, I developed a strong work ethic and a sense of financial independence from my family. That outcome was not foreordained. I could have chosen another path, influenced by others outside of the family or for any number of reasons. Regarding the financial independence part of my character, I absorbed and followed in the footsteps of family. Still, having some judgment and mindfulness about what I saw in my mentors, I chose to deviate from the influence of the social prejudice I observed. I also developed a different philosophy in my thinking about religion than my parents or siblings—not better or worse, just different.

I was talking with a neighbor about some of these thoughts on a walk through our neighborhood one afternoon. He is a couple of years older than I am. When talking about the influence our parents had on us as kids, he made the point that for each of our siblings, our parents were different. You have probably heard or read the theories about the effect on a child's development by birth order, age at entering school, economic influences, and a myriad of other impacts. So, we compared our personal stories as we walked along. I was the firstborn in my family and so had the undivided interest of my parents for five years. He was firstborn, but it was only about eighteen months before a brother was born. He commented that he thought that was too soon. Parents' attention is divided between siblings at that point and the more kids in the family, the smaller the share of one-on-one time. My first five years were spent as the only child, and I had the attention of my adult family to myself. So much of what I became was shaped by that dynamic. My walking friend had that sole attention for less than two years. My brothers, who were born after me, never had it at all. The stories that are remembered by them are more likely to be populated with sibling interaction in addition to adult interaction, and that forms a different family environment and dynamic. This difference in those first few years had effects on their development that are unlike what I experienced. I missed the early sibling interactions since they came later. My brothers had them from the outset.

The parents in each child's life are in a different place in their life with each child. Over time, the parents experience changing work and family responsibilities, different financial circumstances, perhaps a deterioration in health, a divorce, the death of a spouse, and other life events that cause them to present themselves differently to each child. Even though siblings are in the same family, each child is growing up in a different environment. Consider situations where there is a divorce in the young child's life or perhaps the death of both parents requires the child to move in with others— something that happened to my maternal grandmother. There are innumerable variations on the environment influencing each child's development. You will notice in family gatherings when siblings are recounting stories of events that were shared when they were young, there will be discrepancies in the details. All are more or less as accurate as memories can be, but they are remembered from different perspectives.

After talking with a friend, Mia, about the thesis for this book, she told me about being the third girl in a family who wanted a boy. The first two girls in the family were about a year apart in age, maybe three years older. Her family, for a time, lived with grandparents, similar to my situation but with major differences. Her grandmother did not care for her and expressed that dissatisfaction in many ways. An example was when Mia's grandmother, who had a fondness for apples, had several to give to her granddaughters. She had the girls gather to receive their gifts. The largest, shiniest, and most perfect apple she gave to the oldest girl, the next, smaller apple she gave to the next, and then, the last and smallest, not-so-good-looking apple she gave to Mia. She was devastated by how clear the message was about her importance. This story was indicative of the way she was treated as a child. Her grandmother's approval was very important to her, so she was always trying to accomplish something that would impress her—to no avail. She told me she believes that unappreciated place she had in the family caused her to develop a strong competitive streak, trying to stand out in a positive way to the family adults. It was not until she was in her fifties and the grandmother passed away that she finally decided to let her hurt go and forgive her grandmother.

Today, Mia has her own successful business and a husband and daughter she cares for deeply. She is kind, thoughtful, and sincerely cares about the welfare of her friends. This, to me, is a situation where the grandparents, particularly the grandmother, in a child's life were role models but exhibited behaviors that were not good. However, the child did not grow up to emulate their shortcomings but instead lived a life consciously rejecting that behavior and developing a strong-willed, competitive character with a good and caring heart. These experiences in the first few years of life are formative. However, the character being formed is not always one that develops the same, hurtful behaviors to others as they grow into adults, but the child's character may evolve in an opposite direction as a reaction to those early experiences.

My friend's situation is a good example. Mia didn't have the firstborn experience: her parents wanted a boy, and she was a girl; her grandmother exhibited disdain for her; and so the dynamics involved could have caused real problems in her character development. However, Mia strived to improve her situation as a child, trying to prove her worth. That effort led to the development of a strong competitive streak in her character and a rejection of that behavior as acceptable in later life with her own child. That childhood environment could have led to a "victim" mentality, but she rejected that and chose strength and compassion instead.

LAW AND ORDER

THE RULE OF LAW MY GRANDPARENTS experienced in their early years was different in some ways from society today. Then, society was governed by laws but not so many laws as today. Enforcement was often at the discretion of the local town sheriff. The sheriff I knew was an elected official, so he needed to answer to the electorate for his actions. In small towns where most of the town residents knew each other, the sheriff's judgment was often affected by a deep personal knowledge of the people involved in situations they had to deal with.

My grandfather told me a story about when he lived in a small South Carolina town, around 1910. In this town, there lived a man who was known as the town bully and generally despised by the residents. Some event he precipitated led several of the men in the town to call him to meet with them one night. When he arrived, there were about fourteen men present, and one of those men promptly shot and killed him. Shortly after, the town sheriff arrived at the scene and entered the room where the now dead man lay on the floor. As the sheriff entered, he recognized the fourteen men and saw it was the town bully lying dead. The men looked at him without speaking and, with the sheriff watching, slowly passed the gun that was used through all of their hands until the last one standing by a window tossed it outside. The sheriff, comprehending the situation, looked at all of them and said, "I guess I'll never know who actually shot him, will I?" They collectively answered "no" and with that, the situation was resolved.

I can't speak to illegal sales of liquor in cities and how that was handled, but I can give my impression as to how it was handled in a small town I am familiar with in the late 1940s and early 1950s. The sale of illegal liquor was not a sophisticated venture but mostly consisted of small-time "moonshine" operations. My impression was that everyone knew the practice was illegal, but they thought of it almost like a community service—something widely known but not publicly talked about. It seemed that the town population did not consider the operators "criminals" and if they didn't cause any trouble, they were not bothered. It was also generally acknowledged, but never proven, that small payments were made to local law enforcement to keep it that way. Law enforcement helped keep peace in the small town dictated by laws, for sure, but with a practical application. You've no doubt seen movies where a situation like this was exploited by greedy, self-serving officials. That probably happened in some places but not in any I was aware of.

In the case of us youngsters, when we got in some sort of trouble where the police were involved, the local law's first action was to notify our parents of what we had done and have them take care of it. And, in those days, the parents did take care of us, usually more strictly than law enforcement would have. One afternoon, my mother and I heard the doorbell ring. We went to the front of the house and opened the door. Standing there was a very large Georgia state trooper holding my little brother, Lowry, by the back of his shirt. Lowry was probably three or maybe four. The trooper looked at my mother and told her that as he was driving down the street a block from our house, a mudball was thrown and smacked into his cruiser. My brother threw it. The trooper then looked down at my brother and asked him how he would like it if someone threw a mudball at his family's automobile. Lowry looked back at him and said, "We don't have an automobile; we have a Ford!" I think that actually made the trooper smile. He finished his conversation with my mother and left her to explain to Lowry what he had done wrong. I think this episode was an example of true "community policing."

I was involved with several of my teenage friends one Friday night in a situation where the town police observed our preparations and interrupted us before we had done anything we shouldn't have. We had just gotten out of a car—driven by the only one of us old enough to drive—parked near an abandoned drive-in movie theatre. Our intent was to steal some of the post-mounted speakers that had yet to be removed. As we were standing there on the dirt road flanking the old outdoor theatre and finalizing our plan, a police car appeared some hundred yards away. They announced their presence with a loudspeaker, while simultaneously shining a big searchlight toward us. The driver of the car immediately panicked and sped away, with dirt from the road thrown into the air from the back tire and the doors we had left open slamming from the momentum. Abandoned, we all fled through the dark in different directions. Some of the boys tried to hide but were quickly caught, only to give up the names of the rest of us. One of the boys called me later that night to let me know the police had my name and were going to call my parents the next day. That same boy told me that as he was being apprehended, he saw one of the officers draw his weapon and aim at me as I was running across an adjacent highway to the woods beyond. Another officer, he said, yelled to the first one, "Don't shoot! It's just a teenager."

That next day was a Saturday and undoubtedly the longest day of my life, waiting for the phone to ring. I volunteered to rake the yard, which I did, plus any other chores I could think of to try to position myself the best that I could for the reckoning with my parents I knew was to come. Nightfall came and no phone call. In fact, the dreaded call never came. In retrospect, we had not actually committed any actionable offense prior to the police intervention, so I think they knew just the threat of calling my parents would be punishment enough. It was plenty.

There was another occasion involving our small-town police that was just the opposite. My friend and I, I'll call him Bobby, wanted to see a rodeo at the local stadium complex but we had no money for tickets. We were pacing along the cyclone fence topped with barbed wire that encircled the stadium when, it seemed out of nowhere, the police chief stepped up and confronted us from the other side of the fence. Bobby was well known in town as a particularly talented young man and an excellent student but coming from a family who was not in the best financial situation. So, not having money for tickets would not have been a surprise to the chief. He looked at Bobby with an emotionless expression and asked, "Bobby, are you boys looking to jump the fence?" Bobby, to my dismay, sheepishly stared at the ground and said "Yessir." The chief studied the two of us for a moment and, still with no emotion showing, told us to give it about fifteen minutes, and all of his officers would be on the other side of the stadium.

How my parents disciplined me as a child and the fair way I thought it was done with punishments appropriate for the infractions and with the focus on the misdeed, not on my worth as a person, led to my personal views of appropriate law enforcement following a similar pattern. Law enforcement personnel are typically recruited from the area of the community they serve. They are part of the community and usually share the same values, tempered by the oath they swear to uphold the law. My childhood experiences with my parents enforcing good behavior, added to my later youthful experiences with police enforcing the law, had a profound impact on me. I recognize I am human with the frailties that come with that condition but, overall, I believe, just like my parents when I was young, the vast majority of the brothers and sisters in blue strive to the best of their abilities to do the right thing and do it with dignity and compassion, to the extent the circumstances in each individual encounter allow. Later during my career, I had the good fortune to work closely with law enforcement in three different universities where police departments administratively reported to me. My childhood experiences set the tone for a good working relationship.

When I hear the calls for "defunding the police," I see this sentiment as a reaction to localized events, horrible as they are, extrapolated to law enforcement in the nation as a whole. My experience with law enforcement is similar to my experience with large organizations of any type. Individuals in a big group reflect the values of the communities they come from. If the community they were raised in, or lived in for years, has biases for or against certain cultural groups in that community, it will influence their interactions with others in accomplishing their assigned tasks. Sometimes, the influence will guide an unthinking, kneejerk reaction to an emergency situation. The learned community biases will surface in a conflict, favoring some to the detriment of others, when persons in a conflict are different from the officer. Police officers usually are products of the community they are recruited from, so these biases will be present. In police departments, the leadership recognizes this phenomenon and incorporates this knowledge such that the officers are taught through repetitive training activities to enforce the law fairly and without prejudice in all circumstances.

This training, properly done and with examples set by leadership, will guide "muscle memory" in fast moving, emergency situations, where necessary reaction times in life-or-death situations do not allow for contemplation. Smart, consistent, and continuous training will overcome inherent biases in those split-second reactions and lead to positive outcomes. "Defunding" the police is an emotional reaction to a real situation that needs change. It is not a viable strategy in any sense. Demanding change in leadership, training, and professional recruitment practices are what are needed to reduce problems with excessive use of force, leading to unnecessary death or injury. This demand for continuous training and sound leadership has just as much validity in police response to emergencies other than those involving subconscious cultural biases. One, in particular, is the quick and effective response to an active shooter situation. These events strike like a bolt from the blue, and most injury and death come in the first few minutes. An effective police response is typically one provided by a force with competent leadership, appropriate training, and timely, real-time communications as the event unfolds.

One instance at the University of Central Florida began with a shooter pulling the fire alarm in a dormitory to cause multiple targets to flood into the hallway where he intended to begin his carnage. The campus police were immediately on their way to the scene for what they thought was a fire. As they were halfway there, police dispatch alerted them that it was not a fire but an active shooter. They continued to the scene without hesitation, or any surprise, as part of their training had included knowledge that pulling a fire alarm is part of a known game plan for active shooters. Their rapid, unhesitating response allowed them to contain the shooter before he shot anyone other than himself. That response was not luck but the result of excellent leadership, training, and using all available intelligence communicated to them in real time to aid their response.

People sometimes draw law enforcement into a situation in an effort to create a dramatic message for the media. Demonstrations on college campuses are not unusual events. I always appreciated the passion and commitment students showed when demonstrating for causes they believed worthy. And I enjoyed the back and forth I had with leaders of various groups, usually very smart, articulate students. One such leader I related to went on to represent Florida in its House of Representatives.

Demonstrations tend to attract law enforcement and local media. Once, prior to a staged protest, I met with students who I knew were very energized by their cause. They were considering a confrontation with police, with the idea of being arrested and carried off in the presence of TV cameras. They thought this would be an enhancement to great and exciting media coverage of their message. I was pleased to have the opportunity in advance of the event to provide them with some advice for their consideration. I told them that I had no problem at all with their planned demonstration. However, I relayed that I was aware some of them were considering forcing an arrest in front of the cameras covering the event to, in their minds, draw broader coverage and interest in their passion for the cause.

My advice was to consider that an arrest, and possible conviction of a violation of law, would create a permanent record for the perpetrator, something that would follow them for the rest of their life. I strongly suggested they weigh that consequence against their perceived value of the televised public statement they would be making. I said something to the effect that, "If you believe in your cause so much and you think being arrested and hauled off in handcuffs in front of cameras is so important that you are willing to make that sacrifice—then go ahead. But please, at least think about the longer-term consequences to your life before choosing that action." The demonstration went forward with all of the shouting, chants, and placards being waved in the air that make up the show. Police were present, and the cameras were rolling. But none of the students did anything to get arrested. I felt very good about the outcome of that event.

I respect freedom of speech as memorialized in the United States Constitution. I appreciate the right to peaceably assemble, and I certainly admire and respect the passion, energy, and devotion citizens bring to these public demonstrations. I absolutely do not support violence as a part of these events. Violence certainly gets attention and feeds the ego of those responsible, but the result is typically societal condemnation, people get hurt or killed, property is destroyed, and lives are wasted in prison. The organization sponsoring the event and those planning it are held responsible. No matter how "just" the cause, in the end, the cause is tainted in public opinion, and the intended goals often suffer irreversible damage.

⌐⁄⁄\~

Metaphysics and Religion

BELIEF SYSTEMS

WHEN MY MOTHER-IN-LAW, EVA, WAS 101 years old, she told me that even at her age, she still reflected on the time as a child, when she was living in a coal-mining town in Pennsylvania, she woke up in the night and thirstily gulped down a glass of water. She panicked as she realized it was after midnight, the start of a religious day of fasting, and she had some water! For years after, she was convinced she had committed a great sin and would certainly be held accountable for it in the hereafter. Eva lived for years with a sense of guilt over that drink of water. Later in life, she learned more about her religion and its origins and gained more perspective on the teachings of her faith. She began to sense some anger at how much angst she had suffered as a child because of the way she had been indoctrinated to be so fearful of the sinful consequences of any small misstep in her actions.

This simple story of Eva suffering years of despair over a drink of water illustrates the power religion has over the emotions of believers. Different cultures share different religious beliefs and, while most are monotheistic, there are stark differences in how different religions are practiced, how the histories of each are recounted, and in the rules governing the lives of their believers.

"Do you believe in God?" That is a question I've heard many times in my life. The answer expected is yes or no, with some hedging their answer with an "I'm not sure." Giving some thought to the question, I think a reasonable response might be, "What do you mean exactly, by 'God?'" I believe I understand what people mean when they ask that question. They are asking if I believe in the spiritual entity that represents the concept of God, as held in the mind of the questioner. This entity has various forms in the minds of people asking based on their spiritual beliefs and upbringing. Simply agreeing that, yes, I believe in God does not actually mean that the person answering shares the same beliefs as the one asking the question, since they have their own mental picture of God that well may differ from the vision of the person asking.

I am more at ease thinking of God as a Higher Power. I don't think of God as a physical entity that I can visualize in any particular form, as that would imply limitations. This does not mean I discount the idea that a Higher Power would not choose to be seen or understood as an image that would facilitate communication in a particular instance. My thoughts in this area have continued to evolve, as I have learned more about other beliefs and examined my own spirituality over the years. When asked about religion, people tend to narrowly define and put a label on their personal beliefs. The labels are Christian, Muslim, Sikh, atheist, agnostic, or something else. How is this profound choice made?

Children's religious experience, or lack thereof, comes from adults around them. They are ingrained with their beliefs. As children grow into adults and have exposure to a wider view of religion from different viewpoints, life gets complicated. New exposures may echo current beliefs, add nuances, contradict some tenants of an existing belief system, or, possibly wholly reject a belief system held since childhood. Uncomfortable new thoughts will spring up from these exposures that challenge the beliefs inherited as a child. Just having those challenging thoughts may bring on a sense of guilt, since those early beliefs came from trusted people. They came from parents, grandparents, or other significant adults who were looked up to.

Guided by my parents, I became a member of the Methodist church in 1954 when I was ten years old. I didn't have much life experience to make a choice on my own. However, I think it was a good idea because that affiliation stimulated thoughts about religion. Without that exposure, I would have missed hearing basic stories on the foundation of religious thought, the discussions of moral values, and any serious contemplation of the concept of life after death. Death comes to everyone; there is no getting around it. As a young person, death is only a concept, something to consider later, and not something that a young person thinks will happen to them. As one ages, the concept of death starts to become more than a concept and, instead, a reality one does not want to face. That is the norm in my observation of human behavior. However, some do accept that reality and are at peace with it. My brother, Jeffrey, died of cancer. He was very strong in his faith and accepted that he was dying. He did not want to die; he loved his life, but he knew death was inevitable and he accepted it with grace and an attitude of anticipation of what would come next. By the way he accepted the inevitable, he was a role model for my brothers and me. I hope to have his same graceful acceptance of the end when my time comes. I believe I will. My early experiences in the churches I attended laid the groundwork for many thoughtful hours developing my beliefs in this area.

In my twenties and thirties, I attended an Episcopal church on a fairly regular basis. I was assigned one year to be the program chair for a young adult Sunday school class. When I invited a professor to speak to one of the classes about genetic engineering, after the event I was, maybe not surprisingly, no longer asked to provide the programs. I thought the topic would generate a great discussion involving science, religion, morality, and law. Instead, the class just looked at the speaker as some sort of heretic who I had invited to the class for reasons they couldn't fathom. I was struck by how being challenged to confront and discuss an idea alien to the expected retelling of the same, old ideas would spark such a backlash. This observation proved to be telling of human reaction to receiving information that counters long-held beliefs or that challenges one to consider alternatives to the status quo. When a person is in a comfort zone in the way they see the world, there is a strong desire to not let this zone be disrupted. If a person is not in a favorable situation in life, there is a fervent hope for change.

Both situations exist within society and are strongly evidenced in the push and pull over activities in everyday life. In the working world, dissatisfaction with working conditions or compensation result in a push for unionization. Those who are satisfied with the status quo resist unionization out of concern it may disrupt their equilibrium. In elections, voters vote either for change or to keep everything as is. If left to play out with arguments publicly posited on both sides of differences, eventually the condition of humanity will be improved. My experience in the Sunday school class showed me how vehemently people react at the first questioning of long-held beliefs. I would wager that as time has passed, if the ideas presented that Sunday were the topic for discussion in a meeting in that same church today, the reaction would be quite different because more public discussion of these ideas have taken place in the time since then. People need a little time and space to absorb information that leads to changes in attitudes and beliefs. People just don't react well to new ideas when first presented. This is a lesson I learned and used in my working career. When change was needed, it required explanation, discussion, and time to be contemplated and absorbed.

Once while I was active in the Episcopal church, I was invited to be part of the Bishop's Advisory Council on the ministry's team to interview applicants interested in studying for the ministry. I asked our priest why I was asked to be a part of that team, as my ecclesiastical knowledge was minimal at best. I was told it was because of my position at a college. He believed that I could offer the team an opinion as to whether the applicants would measure up in a college environment based on my experience with college students. I'll admit I was worried about that answer. The interviews took place on a Saturday in Charlottesville, Virginia, so I rode with the priest over the mountains from where we lived in the Shenandoah Valley for the day of interviews. We left very early in the morning and as we were coming to the top of Afton Mountain in a heavy morning fog, the priest dozed off and headed toward the guardrail at the edge of a mountain cliff. I grabbed the wheel and kept us on the road as he jerked awake and regained control of the steering wheel.

After that little adrenaline surge, the rest of the drive was uneventful. Once at our destination, to my surprise, I believe

I had some good input for the team after my interviews of the applicants. I found it very interesting to hear the various reasons why different people felt a desire to serve and how they presented their case. Fortunately, the other interview team members were focused on the religious motivations, and I only had to opine on their presentations to the extent I believed they could handle the academics. This experience listening to the religious views they expressed, even though not my role to evaluate, gave me a lot to think about. Each person interviewed was sincere in their desire to join the ministry, passionate in their beliefs but had different perspectives on the same religious order.

A disparity in perspective of religious beliefs is common among people I have encountered. Members of a given religion, passionate in their beliefs, often express differing details of their understanding of their religion. This variation in interpreting and expressing views on a religious subject is consistent with expressions of belief in non-religious topics as well—people interpret what they read, hear, and see based on the context of experiences in their life. Immanuel Kant, an eighteenth-century German philosopher observed something to the effect that the mind does not conform to things, but things conform to the mind. Put another way, we achieve an understanding of what we experience based on what we believe we are experiencing and not necessarily based on the reality of what we are experiencing.

It is healthy to hear varied viewpoints on a subject, particularly if a person is open to evolving their own beliefs as a result of contemplating and evaluating something heard that deviates from their understanding. Over the years, during conversation, I've found myself negatively reacting to a point being made by another person.

Then later, contemplating what was said that I totally disagreed with, I realize that maybe I didn't completely understand their intended meaning because I had filtered what I was hearing through my existing view of the world. When I thought more openly about what was said, I gained a broader understanding of the topic I had rigidly disagreed with. That openness sometimes caused a change in my thinking. My brother, David, is licensed to perform wedding ceremonies, which he does, and occasionally delivers the Sunday sermons at his church. During conversations about happenings in our daily life, he will sometimes refer to a Bible verse to help make a point. I don't always get his point at first, as I take what he quoted literally. But as he explains his understanding of the message delivered in the verse, his point then makes sense to me. By reconsidering my initial skepticism by keeping an open mind to the thoughtful, metaphorical explanation of the quoted verse, his point took on a new meaning.

"What I meant to say was. . ." is a phrase often heard as people struggle to find the right words to express their thoughts. This is a sign of the difficulty people have in sometimes finding the words to convey a thought to another person without being misunderstood. I have learned to listen for the intended meaning in another's statements rather than allowing myself to be too literal in interpreting what is being said. Body language, facial expressions, eye movements, and intonation all need to be evaluated for meaning in an exchange of thoughts. These are physical manifestations of communication, often more telling than the words being spoken. Not being present to see the body language that went with the original spoken words memorialized in religious texts contributes to misinterpretation and variations in interpretation of the speaker's intended meaning. In most, if not all, of the established religions in the world, the first stories told were oral, with all of the associated body language as part of the communication. Later, when the stories were recorded, only the words remained—the body language critical to telling the story, lost.

Today, when religious leaders tell the old stories to their followers, they add *their* body language to the telling. Not even being alive to hear and see the original of the stories as they were orated, they make up their own inflections in tone and body language and often simply display emotional theatre. The words may be the same, but the original meaning of the stories may change. However, to the astute listener, the very original meaning may still be discerned. But to the less astute, the original meaning can be transformed by the body language of the contemporary speaker into something very different from the original intent of the story. And, adding to the strong possibility for misinterpretation are the subtle changes in meanings of the words in the stories brought about through translations from one language to another. Aramaic to English is an example.

As a young child, my parents had me attend Sunday school and say prayers every night with their coaching. In those prayers, I asked for God's protection and for blessings on my family and anyone else on a given night I might want to add. My parents instilled in me a sense of right and wrong and the basic idea of the Golden Rule: do unto others as you would have them do unto you. They didn't delve into deep dogma or have me memorize scripture. From that upbringing, I developed a sense of fair play and treating others well—at least as well as a child can do, which is not always consistent. I was getting the idea that my actions were being observed and judged by a vague concept I had of God. As I got older, I think that general approach to my spiritual upbringing mitigated some of the guilt I felt when I questioned some of the tenets of the faith I was raised in. Lying in bed at night during my teenage years, I thought how comforting it would be if I could just accept the teachings of my church without question. But I had questions. I couldn't put those questions out of my mind, not a total rejection of the teachings but questions about the particulars in the sermons and stories.

The upbringing I had was completely different from my mother-in-law, who was subjected to a much more rigorous specificity and admonition about how, as she put it, any deviation from the church teachings was a serious sin. She told me one morning that in her old age, she had finally reached a place where she was free from religion. Surprised, I asked what she meant by that after all the years of expressing to me her belief in God. What she went on to explain was that she had achieved peace through a growing sense of personal connection to the Almighty, as she referred to God, as opposed to having controlling church intermediaries between her and God telling her what to believe and conveying to her that God expected her to adhere to the rules these intermediaries set forth. She said it took her many years to shake off the guilt that burdened her, as she internally questioned some of the expectations others laid on her to believe as they did. When her life experiences gave her doubts about some of the rules her church imposed, it caused an inner turmoil: a struggle between emotional guilt for questioning the rules versus what she was reasonably seeing in life with her own eyes.

As my mother-in-law aged, it was not surprising that she thought of dying, of coming to the end of her life and what, if anything, would come next for her. In our conversations, she expressed a very strong belief in God. Her faith in God never wavered. What did waver was her belief in many of the details of the religious teachings she received as a child about a life after death. She wanted to believe what she was told but sometimes, she expressed to me, she thought that maybe there is only nothingness afterward. That uncertainty caused her to be afraid. In this state, she did not doubt the existence of God; she just didn't know what God's plan for humanity was after death, even though her religious training assured her of the existence of heaven.

Eva's ambivalence is common. I have been with relatives who consider themselves to be Christians and have comported themselves through life adhering to a Christian way of life. When death is perceived to be at a distance, faith in an afterlife is strong. Yet when death is coming near, doubt grows about what comes next. I have also been around relatives who were ill and knew their time was finished, accepted the fact that death comes to us all, and faced it without fear, comforted by their belief in an afterlife. I admire that. Even so, I understand the trepidation in the others. When all the signs indicate that the end is near, some find it necessary to confess their entire perceived, and real, shortcomings to family members around them. There is, at that point, no consideration for the feelings and emotions of the family members that are the recipients of the outpouring of these "last rite" revelations. The world shrinks to the space of their dimming existence. I am not suggesting this is wrong, I'm saying that it is not unusual, and family members need to be prepared for this phenomenon and accept it without judgment. This is a period when family members closest to those near the end struggle with the question posed by doctors and hospital personnel as to how far they should go with extreme efforts to prolong that person's life. These questions are intense, troubling, and often take place when the family members are emotionally stressed to their limits. I'm not convinced there is a "right" answer to that question, because each person confronted with the question comes to it depending, to some extent, on the closeness of the relationship, the strength of the love between them, and the conflict between accepting the end is very near and the overwhelming desire to keep them alive. The best counsel in this time of stress and trouble comes from my wife, who once said to me that we should keep in mind that whatever the outcome, we all do the best we can in dealing with these situations. Faith is a belief in something that cannot be experienced with the senses. It is a concept embraced by the mind. Without the reinforcement of experiencing any physical manifestations of the belief during life, the strength of the belief will ebb for some when the Grim Reaper is at the door.

I admire, even envy to some extent, people who are comfortable in their faith, and I have no interest in trying to dissuade them from their beliefs. However, I struggle with the idea that each of their philosophies is the only true way to understanding or that their beliefs are the only correct beliefs. I'm reminded of the old story of several blind men approaching an elephant for the first time and attempting to discern what this beast looks like. Each of the blind men touched a different part of the elephant, coming up with very different impressions. One touched the elephant's trunk and exclaimed, "The elephant resembles a big snake!" Another touched the elephant's broad side and said, "No, it's like a wall!" Another of the blind men felt one of the elephant's legs and said, "Surely, this creature is similar to a big tree. I can feel the tree's trunk!" Each part of the elephant that was touched was real but without knowledge of the whole, the impression by part was misleading.

As religious beliefs developed over millennia in different geographies, with vast space between groups of people, there was little to no merging of independently developed religious thought with that developed by other groups far away. Many of the first stories of religious experiences were passed down through generations by word of mouth, with resulting variations on the original stories of the beginnings of life. If different religious beliefs are stripped to their fundamental cores, those fundamentals will likely be found to be essentially the same, only obscured through the ages by variations in the retelling of those stories compounded by misinterpretation by the listeners. Each time a story is told, it is told from the perspective of the person telling it. A person listening to a story interprets the story based within the context of their life experiences.

The Navaho have a belief in kachinas as spirit intermediaries between them and the Great Spirit. Christians have a belief in angels as spirit intermediaries between them and God. The details are significantly different but at the core of both is a belief in spirit intermediaries. This is one, small example of commonalities in religions but expressed very differently. Therefore, I am not inclined to condemn any person's belief as misguided, since each probably contains some true elements of the whole. I will continue my path in search of further enlightenment and I, like others, will always be influenced in my interpretations by the way I see the world through the lenses shaped by my past experiences. I am happy that I had an introduction to a Higher Power in my early years but not to the point of extinguishing my ability to think for myself, to question what I don't understand, or to seek my own way in attempting to find clarity.

The more I experience life, the more I learn about my existence and the more I am in awe of the power, force, complexity, and infinite creativity in and around us. I am amazed how little humans appreciate the ultimate gift of being alive, even if only for a speck of time in infinity. It makes me unbelievably sad to know how many lives are shortened through wars and other horrors we inflict upon ourselves. A life of seventy, eighty, or even a hundred years is as brief in the span of eternity as the flash of light from a firefly on a summer night. Yet humans find ways, like war, to make even this short experience with life even shorter still. Disturbingly, many times religion is used to justify a war that leads to the premature end to millions of lives. "Doing God's will," is sometimes put forth as justification for this horrible practice or using war as tool to "purify" humanity in some way—as if God needs human help to eliminate a certain segment of society. These same advocates of working to achieve God's will express their belief in an "all powerful" deity that they are helping. An all-powerful deity, by definition, does not need help from humans to achieve goals. Maybe humans are used to "help" as a means to some other end having to do with evolution of the human spirit but not because the help is needed to accomplish something an all-powerful deity cannot achieve directly. These professed needs to "help" God achieve goals comes from an ancient belief, still present in some quarters today, that there are multiple gods who are in competition for the worship of all humanity. They also come from religious leaders with influence in governmental affairs who invoke their god to justify personal goals which, oftentimes, are not in sync with the actual principles of the religion they falsely claim to represent.

When I admit my inability to fully understand the enormity of even the concept of a Higher Power, I don't mean it in a negative sense. I view this recognition as a step toward understanding. Enlightenment starts with openness to new thoughts, recognition that there are things unknown, and a desire to know and understand. For perspective on fully comprehending the enormity of a Higher Power, let me show my lack of comprehension of something less significant that falls *under the domain* of a Higher Power. That is the concept of infinity and the existence of a universe in infinity. The currently predominant, but certainly not only, explanation for the creation of the universe, as perceived in the last hundred years, is summed up in the "Big Bang" theory. The English astronomer, Fred Hoyle, coined this term in 1949 to describe an ongoing discussion regarding a hypothesis that all matter in the universe was created at one specific time. An explosion of energy came from a central point, ultimately creating all the matter in the universe— the stars, planets, and other elements inhabiting it.

When I say, "the creation of the universe," I find myself, perhaps primitively, thinking about the universe as some finite space, much as people in ancient times thought in a limited way of the Earth as the center of existence, with the myriad circling stars seen as mysterious lights in the heavens having as many explanations for their meaning, origins, and purpose as there were cultures. I tell myself that the universe is not a finite space but boundless. Yet, even as I tell myself that, I can't quite grasp what that means. Boundaries, limits, measurable distances, maps, stories of definable kingdoms, countries, and even the idea of heaven and hell as specific places closely associated with Earth have defined my life. It's tough to get past a lifetime of thinking a certain way.

Where did this enormous energy described in the Big Bang theory, creating the countless stars and other phenomena in our skies, come from? If the concept of infinity means no beginning, then applying that notion to our universe presents a conundrum. The Big Bang, then, may not have been the start of our universe but something that repeats in an endless continuum, reusing the same energy. Further, if there are no boundaries to space, it is infinite, why should there not be other "big bangs" occurring beyond ours? Or maybe the matter came through some portal connecting to an alternate or parallel universe. Human understanding of the physics and composition of the universe is progressing at a rapid rate. More powerful telescopes are being launched into the vastness of space, greater computing power is enabling faster processing of the data received from exploration of the moon and planets, and data received from satellites and sensory devices launched from Earth and traveling millions of miles away are continuously adding to our knowledge.

This new knowledge challenges—and, in some cases, invalidates—earlier theories about the makeup and origin of what we profess to know about the universe. The Big Bang theory may be looked back on by future generations with a smile and a nod as to how little their ancestors actually knew. I struggle to comprehend infinity and all that goes with it. The concept of a higher or greater power that is a more complex concept than infinity means I have a long way to go on this journey of pursuing enlightenment. I will, however, continue my quest to learn more and, in so doing, gain personal fulfillment as my perspective and faith in the existence of a power I cannot currently explain grows over time. This journey seeking enlightenment is truly fulfilling in both a secular and spiritual sense.

I have just explained my struggle to comprehend the enormity of the universe, much less to comprehend the specifics of an overarching Higher Power. So, how can I choose a very specific religious belief to label myself with and say this is what I believe to the exclusion of all other possibilities? However, it is clear to me that humans have not advanced in development as life forms capable of multi-dimensional, limitless thinking, let alone being able to comprehend what is incomprehensible in their present state. That does not mean people should cease trying—far from it. I continue to strive for understanding by keeping an open mind to clues I am given in my daily life. Clues come in the form of experiences or events that cannot be explained by my current knowledge of how the world works.

About a mile from where my paternal grandparents lived on the St. Marys River lies a private cemetery, nestled under huge live oaks festooned with Spanish moss and surrounded by brushy woodland, allowing limited rays of sunlight to penetrate through. A number of local families have been interned there dating back to the late 1800s, including members of my family. This cemetery is the site of an experience I can only describe as transcendental. When I was very young, I met a boy a few years older than me. His name was Freeman Groover. He was the son of a man who lived nearby who worked with my uncle. Several years later, I heard that Freeman, who could not swim but loved to fish, did not return home one day, and his empty boat was found floating along the river. Without hearing much more about it, I presumed he had drowned.

In 2010, I was at a graveside service at that cemetery on the bank of the St. Marys River. The service was for my uncle, Charles. As the service ended and people were gathering in small groups or in the process of leaving, I felt a presence over my shoulder. I turned to see who it was. The man standing there, smiling at me, said, "Hey Billy, remember me? Freeman Groover." It surprised me because I was under the belief that he had drowned in the river some years before. I didn't say that. In fact, I don't recall what I may have said in reply to him, but I know I didn't reveal I thought he was dead. But it seemed obvious at the time that I was wrong. I don't recall anyone else being in the immediate vicinity, and I don't remember the meeting ending or us parting company. It was very brief. He seemed happy and smiling. That's it.

In the following years, as I told different people about the encounter and how spooky it was to have someone approach me in the cemetery who I thought had drowned years earlier, I continued to believe I was misinformed about the drowning. Then, in 2020, I was in that same cemetery under those big oak trees attending a service for my aunt, Dawn. The service ended and as we were preparing to leave, my wife, Ksenia, my brother, Lowry, and my sister-in-law, Beverly, began talking to one of the women from the funeral home. She was packing up the chairs and other supplies used at the service. I brought up my encounter with Freeman years earlier at this same cemetery and how I was mistaken about his death. She looked quite surprised. *He did drown*, she told me. She added some of the details about him and then turned and pointed to a spot, about five or so yards away from where we were standing, to show me his grave. He died in 2006 when he was sixty-six years old. Yet, he appeared to me in that cemetery, in 2010.

I don't recall anyone being in our immediate presence at the encounter those years before—we were standing alone. I remember how radiant Freeman looked. I don't mean he was emitting light or anything like that. I mean he looked calm, relaxed, and smiling, as if he had not a care in the world. He looked to be in his early thirties with light brown hair. There were no signs of any stress at all in his face. He was happy. Ksenia remembers me telling her of the encounter the day it happened. She didn't witness what I saw but she thought it strange I hadn't introduced her, since I was consistent in introducing her to people she didn't know at events. Maybe some of the experiences I had as a child with people I call "different" and the stories about life I heard in those days prepared me in some way for this experience. But that encounter shredded my doubt about supernatural forces, even though I can't prove their existence.

I did have occasion to drive by that same cemetery one night in 2021. As I drove by on the rutted dirt road under the trees flanking the cemetery, I glanced through an opening in the brush and trees toward where some of the tombstones were located. In that brief glance into the darkness shrouding the area, I saw four or five small, dim greenish-blue lights hovering above the ground near some of the gravestones. I did not stop. If anything, I may have sped up a little. Thinking later about what I saw, I rationalized that the lights could have been reflections caused by the glow of my passing headlights in the eyes of a group of raccoons or some other animals gathered there. The weakness in my rationalization was not lost on me, being as my car headlights weren't shining in the direction of the hovering lights.

Another event I cannot explain occurred in the time following my father's death. Friends sent Ksenia and me a live Phalaenopsis orchid in a vase, filled with blooms, accompanied by a note expressing their condolences. They knew my wife and I liked orchids and usually had several in our house. We put this gift vase with the orchid on a plant stand in our dining room, near a window that received indirect sunlight, perfect for orchids. All the blooms on this orchid died in the following three or four months, which is not an unusual life span, *except* for three of the blooms. These three blooms continued to thrive, showing no signs of failing, unlike any experience I had ever had with orchid bloom longevity. One year later, during the anniversary week of my father's death, these three orchid flowers abruptly died and dropped from the plant. I took that as a message.

These two events do not mean that I now have specific answers or special insights. However, for me, these events created a sense of awe for how little my temporal knowledge has prepared me for understanding the spiritual dimension to my existence. This overwhelming wonder inspires me to continue to dig deeper, to understand more about the Higher Power that some call God, Yahweh, the Great Spirit, Allah, or any of several other names. An argument against the existence of a Higher Power is that belief typically relies on faith, a conviction that is argued cannot be proven in a scientific way or proven through an experience with the human senses. The encounter with Freeman Groover is one I cannot prove happened in any scientific way, but I know it happened. So, it is one of the reasons I say, "Yes, I believe in a Higher Power," when the question comes. I further believe that forces that come from that power have great influence over my life—and the fact that I even have a life at all.

On a lighter note, there is a simple story, sometimes unwittingly told as a joke, which captures the essence of unseen and misunderstood forces in life. The story takes place in a town that is experiencing a life-threatening flood. As the floodwaters began inundating the town, the local authorities gave evacuation orders, and the residents began leaving. One man, professing a faith in God and a belief that God would take care of him, refused to leave his home when all around him were evacuating. A car driven by a police officer came to his house to take him to higher ground. He refused the offer, stating he had faith God would take care of him.

As the floodwaters continued their rise, the first floor of his two-story home was engulfed. As he retreated to the second floor, a neighbor came by in a boat and offered him a ride out of the area. He again refused, saying that God would take care of him. Finally, he was forced to the roof, as the second floor of his house surrendered to the rising waters. On the roof, a rescue helicopter approached him. The man waved off the helicopter, saying he didn't need the help; God would provide.

A little later, the floodwaters rose above the roof level of his house and after a futile struggle against the powerful floodwaters, he drowned. Afterward, he found himself in heaven facing God. The confused and shaken man asked God, "Why, why did you abandon me to drown after I had put all of my faith in you to take care of me?" To this, God replied, "I sent a car, a boat, and a helicopter. What more did you want?"

ENLIGHTENMENT

IN A METAPHORICAL SENSE, ENLIGHTENMENT IS shining a light of awareness and understanding into areas heretofore dark with ignorance. Philosophers have used the word enlightenment to describe freedom from outside influences to use one's own reason to see what really is and have the courage to express what is seen. Emmanuel Kant was one who expressed that a lack of courage was present in failure to achieve personal enlightenment. Through the pages of history, scientific research has brought light into areas that had been shrouded in superstition. To challenge beliefs that had existed for generations based on observable scientific evidence would seem to be a simple proposition, but it is not. This difficulty arises from a reluctance to part with the status quo—with an ingrained sense of what is, ingrained over years, to change a way of thinking and accept that the old way was not valid. Somehow, admitting to oneself that a lifetime of thinking and acting on beliefs that are proven wrong when confronted with evidence to the contrary is too much to accept when it occurs. Sometimes, it takes years, even generations, for new ways of thinking about life to be absorbed and become part of a person's belief system.

Some answers to questions in life aren't easily found through science or the application of logic. Your personal values, your sense of right and wrong, and determining what is morally and ethically acceptable behavior is not always easy to comprehend. Enlightenment sometimes comes by forcing a realistic interpretation of life as you experience it. To do so takes self-discipline, consciously and deliberately thinking through events in your life and making your own assessment as to what you learned from those events, and not allowing others to interpret the meaning of those events for you. Sadly, many people do not do this. Traveling to new places, having social interactions with people of cultures other than yours, and accumulating a vast store of knowledge can be eye-opening experiences, but they don't automatically trigger enlightenment. Enlightenment comes from developing a personal sense of the meaning of life and your place in it. It's based on examining your personal experiences and thinking through what impact those experiences have on creating your personal worldview. This sense of life and its meaning is an individual phenomenon, not some universal view everyone shares. It comes to you individually from all of life's experiences and, critically, how mindful you are about the impact of those experiences on how life is viewed.

Starting with birth, you are inundated with sights, sounds, taste, smell, and touch, all creating experiences through those five senses. These senses begin to immediately inform you about your environment. Childhood experiences form a base of understanding of the world around you. That base is then enlarged and enhanced as time passes and more of life is experienced. All the stories I have told—and my observations—form the substance of what used to independently think through the realities in my life in pursuit of finding enlightenment along the way. Having a level of skepticism in absorbing the daily messaging that bombards society is helpful. Another way of saying this is developing what is described in the oft-used phrase "critical thinking." Evaluating the merits of the content of this messaging should be based on confidence in the integrity of the source and a personal test of reasonableness. The evaluation importantly needs to shut out the cacophony of demands of others in society telling you what to believe.

For me, the experience of enlightenment is not something that comes in a flash but over time in bits and pieces. My positive feeling about nature that began stirring when I was on that grape arbor as a child have only been amplified over time. The more I experience the natural environment, the more I appreciate what a wonder it is. In the context of the span of a human life, the laws of the natural environment seem fixed, giving a sense of stability. Human nature is not so stable but is more mercurial, changing with emotion and varying from one person to another, making it difficult, but not impossible, to find stability in relationships. That may be why, when those stable relationships are achieved, they are so rewarding. If the Age of Enlightenment prioritized reason as the path to understanding over myth and superstition, that is good guidance in understanding the natural world. But it falls short in attaining enlightenment in human relationships. These are much more difficult to achieve and to maintain. But when such relationships are achieved, they are the most satisfying of all.

—✳—

Aesthetics and Taste

INSPIRATIONS AND CHOICES

FOR MOST OF MY WORKING LIFE, I was involved in various ways with construction. In the military, my training before Officer Candidate School (OCS) was in combat engineering. In OCS, the training was designed to have me commissioned as an officer in the Army Corps of Engineers. Upon graduation, the Vietnam War was winding down and the need for engineer officers was declining. Except for graduates who had received engineering degrees in college, the rest of us were offered a limited choice of other branches. I chose the Quartermaster Corps because it was the closest field to business, which was the career field I planned to go into upon discharge from the army; that led to additional training in finance and other aspects of duty as a quartermaster officer. However, I had already received that earlier training in engineering.

When I left the army and began my forty-six-year career in college and university administration, for about eighty percent of those years I was responsible, among other assignments, for the construction and maintenance of the campus infrastructure. I worked with architects, engineers, and contractors. I was in frequent contact with tradespeople, such as painters, carpenters, electricians, and plumbers. I was also heavily involved in the financial planning to support those operations—from annual budgets for maintenance to planning for the debt to finance construction. Millions of dollars for maintenance and hundreds of millions for construction were involved. I was always comfortable in that environment. It seemed like a career I was meant to be in. Now, I look back at my beginnings and see an obvious relationship. The trail of breadcrumbs in this respect is clear.

Dad was involved in finance in his final months in the army in World War II. His next job for a short time was in the finance department of a railroad company and then he became the bookkeeper for a lumber business, ultimately becoming the majority stockholder and president. I went with him as a young teenager on their last big timber-cutting operation in a forest. As I was growing up, it was not unusual for me to visit the lumber yard and sawmill operations with my dad to see how wood went from being a tree in a forest, through the sawmill to cut and dress the lumber, then the dry kiln treatment for some of it, and finally the retailing of the finished products to carpenters. I worked in the summers for him in that business while I was in high school. That involved loading lumber trucks and, as the business expanded into other building materials, including paint, I was part of the labor force unloading boxcars, stacking lumber, and occasionally filling orders for customers in the trades. In his limited spare time, Dad accomplished many building projects in our home, including constructing an addition to our house.

Grandfather Keefe was assigned engineering tasks in the military during World War I and was a professional painter afterward, working in a naval shipyard, followed by occasional work as a house painter in his older retirement years. I essentially grew up with construction all around me and I was involved with people in the construction industry. The army training was a fortunate surprise, since I thought I would be assigned as a ground pounder in the infantry but I ended up in engineering and quartermaster work. Dad's early time as a bookkeeper was evident to me as a kid when I would see him in our home periodically updating our family's financial records. For a few months after I left the army, I assisted him with bookkeeping duties at his business. So, it came as no surprise that for several years during my career in higher education, one of my roles was as a chief financial officer. My earliest years were spent in the company of my dad and grandfather, both of whom were involved with the finance and construction world. I have no doubt my experiences during those times are the reason I was so comfortable with similar responsibilities in my career.

EXTRAORDINARY EXPERIENCES

A FAMILY AUTOMOBILE TRIP, WHEN I was around ten years old, was to visit my wealthy Great Aunt Lottie Mae who lived in Panama Beach, Florida. I only met her that one time, but the experience opened my eyes to a lifestyle of which I had very little knowledge. Her house was built in colonial style with big columns on a front porch overlooking the beach and the Gulf of Mexico. She had a grand piano in a large living room, along with at least one life-sized marble statue, and oriental carpets everywhere. Dinner service was with beautiful porcelain dishes, silver serving pieces, and elegant silver tableware. I think that visit spurred me to begin considering what lifestyle I should aspire to.

Some other relatives I had not met before were spending the weekend in her big house as well. Three of them were boys about my brother Lowry's age. Late in the afternoon, Dad and I heard yelling in the yard in back. We saw from our second-floor bedroom window that the three little boys were attacking my brother with stripped tree branches they were wielding like fighting sticks. Lowry was standing on a small, raised area, valiantly holding his own and fighting back with his own stick. Dad and I rushed down and broke it up. I, probably unfairly, generalized that this must be what all little rich kids were like—spoiled brats. I believe that influenced me to think about what I might be like if I ever achieved some level of wealth. I certainly didn't want to be like those kids.

A different experience later that afternoon was meeting a young lady who I understood was a distant cousin. She was in a conversation with my great aunt in the living room and I joined them. She was from a South American country; I think Brazil or Argentina but I'm not sure which. She was about twenty years old, strikingly beautiful, and very nice in conversation with me. One side of her face was paralyzed—it looked almost as if it were frozen. Somehow, that only added an element of mystery to her beauty. I was quite infatuated as she was a person totally unlike anyone I had ever met before. My great aunt had a family reputation for favoring her female relatives. I now suspect this was because my aunt was a person of means in a time when females were not treated as equals to their male counterparts. I think she worked to balance that by doing what she could, and it was considerable, for her young female relatives like the one she had introduced me to. I liked that aspect of her character. The weekend came to a close and we left for home.

Spending that time with interesting people in that stunning place was an introduction to a way of life that was rare to me. It was very thought-provoking for years after.

I had similar feelings when, on a family vacation in Florida, we stopped by Jekyll Island and took a tour of the historic Jekyll Island Club grounds, including a visit to the "cottage" that had been a winter getaway for the Rockefeller family prior to World War I. My wife and I have been to Jekyll Island numerous times since for long weekends but, at that early time in my life, the Rockefeller house had not been restored to the level it is now. Some of the original carpets, drapes, and curtains were still in evidence in an elegant but somber Victorian style. Some of the bedrooms I peeked in were being used for storage of elegant old furniture and kitchenware. The lifestyle that was represented piqued my imagination and no doubt affected my thinking about what these people's careers must have been like to afford such a lifestyle. The story of this trip, I'm sure, was a further catalyst in determining to go to college and pursue a career that would allow me to create an environment for myself and future family that was more than I had experienced in my life before.

Materialistic thinking, I suppose, but, hey, it is what it is. That Jekyll experience and my great aunt's way of living were motivating to me. Perhaps in some way associated with these observances, I grew to like antiques. But I have a real aversion to antiques that are in poor condition, broken, or generally in a state that makes current use problematic. I've asked myself why I feel somewhat depressed looking at what was a very fine piece of furniture in its heyday but, through neglect or misuse, is now a sad representation of what it once was. The reason, I have decided, is that this neglected, cast-aside piece of furniture is a metaphor for a way of life that was once grand and has now undeservedly lost its significance.

I have told the story of visiting my great aunt and the visits to Jekyll Island as having a huge impression on my view of the world. There is another decade in my life that had a greater influence. This time was in association with my visits to the Merck grandparents' house on the St. Marys River, a river that separates South Georgia from North Florida. One of my uncles, Walter, a brother to my dad, worked as caretaker for the property of Alicia Guggenheim on the St. Marys River. During this period, her property and my grandparents' property were the only inhabited land on that particular bluff of the river. She had two thousand acres, and my grandparents owned several hundred. I believe there may have been one small landowner in between but during the time of my story, no one lived there and there were no structures on that intervening property.

Uncle Walter's job involved caring for Mrs. Guggenheim's fabulous hunting lodge, several horses, a herd of beef cattle, woodlands, hunting dogs, a boathouse on the river for a mahogany Chris-Craft ski boat powered by a 250-horsepower inboard Cadillac engine, a clay tennis court, and other assorted outbuildings, including a carriage house for a surrey and a larger carriage. Mrs. Guggenheim spent most of her time in New York and abroad, but this was her favorite spot to get away. My uncle would pick her up at the airport in Jacksonville, Florida, and they would drive back to the river estate. He had worked with her horses, training them to provide a number of tasks, like pulling her surrey and her carriage, which the horses didn't much care to do since the experience was so infrequent. Some horses were just for riding pleasure and others were trained to herd the cattle that needed to be moved from one pasture to another.

My involvement in some of this was during the time around 1953 to 1962. On my frequent visits to my grandparents' land nearby, I would sometimes spend time with Uncle Walter and his children, Stephen and Lisa, on the Guggenheim property, where the cottage they lived in was located. During the down times when there were no official visitors, my uncle would allow me to ride with him, and sometimes my dad and Lowry went along to exercise the horses. He would need to take the big Chris-Craft boat out from time to time so we would go with him too. One of the items in the boathouse was an aquaplane, a wooden device designed somewhat like a wide, short surfboard, with two ropes affixed to the top, one for each hand, and a long tow rope underneath to attached to the back of the boat similar to a ski rope. We placed our feet on a rubber mat affixed to the backend of the board—with no straps, boots, or anything. We would lie on the board until the boat picked up speed, which was almost instantaneous, and then stand and steer with the two hand ropes. Sometimes, we would use conventional skis, but the aquaplane had its unique ride that made it really appealing to me.

Horseback riding was always an adventure. Since the horses were not ridden that much, because of the infrequent times Mrs. Guggenheim or her guests were staying at the estate, they were always a little stubborn as they left the stables for rides down the dirt roads and through the woods. However, on the return trips, they were always anxious to get back, so they loved to gallop that same part of the journey. An annoying feature of the ride back was their tendency to try to scrape us off their backs as we galloped near a tree or gatepost. They never succeeded, though it wasn't for lack of trying. Two of the horses were Norwegian Fjords. While sometimes called ponies, they seemed almost the same size as most of the other horses to me. They had some interesting ploys to surprise their riders. Being ridden was something they were trained to do but they didn't like it.

Their names were Sugar and Candy, sweet names that were very misleading. I rode both several times, so I learned their tricks. Sugar would be smoothly running along and then suddenly throw her head back to smack the rider in the face. Being aware of that little trick, I always rode with my head slightly cocked to one side so I wouldn't be hit. Candy had a trick that was harder to deal with. She would be running along and suddenly plant her two front feet and duck her head. You can guess the result for the rider. Once, I was riding her barebacked and she pulled that stunt on me. I went flying over her head, landing in the dirt road. I admit that the action angered me, so I did not let go of the reins when I went over her head and hit the ground. She began backing up, pulling me along, which I think surprised her. I got back on, and we returned to the stables without a reoccurrence of that gambit.

One year when Uncle Walter was moving a herd of cattle from one pasture to another, he let me come along and join him and his team for the move. He had me ride his quarter horse, Tony, that was experienced at driving cattle. When a steer would bolt from the herd, Tony would instantly move to intercept and drive the steer back. All I had to do was hold on and pretend to be a cowboy. One of my favorite horses on the estate was called Sunset Sue. She was a roan that stood seventeen hands high. She was a little older and gentler, so riding her was a very relaxing pleasure. On the opposite end of the spectrum was a horse named Blue because of his blue-black coat. He was a mean-tempered one and, as a result, I never saw anyone ride him, although I know that sometimes happened. Other horses had scars from his kicks or bites. As I was standing on the wooden rail of the corral one day, he came near me, so I decided to give him a friendly little caress on his forehead. As I reached my hand out, I saw his ears go back—not a good sign—so I jerked my hand back just as he moved his head forward to bite it. I literally heard the teeth clack shut where my hand had been a millisecond before. I left him alone after that. Uncle Walter was very cautious about not abusing his position by having my brother and me participate in some of these activities, but I know he liked our help in periodically exercising the horses.

The experiences in the surroundings created by Mrs. Guggenheim had a similar, but more profound, effect on me than my visits to my great aunt's and Jekyll Island. My Guggenheim estate memories paint a picture of the place and the activity that I was fortunate to be around in those days and serves to add to the foundational background that explains how I see the world today. Many things impressed me about her property, which included a magnificent hunting lodge especially designed for the wooded, river-view site. It was a clapboard building with brick foundations, porch, steps, and walkways. The house was painted a gray color that was similar to the gray found in the bark of the nearby oak trees. She had an artist from New York hand paint a simulated lichen growth about a half-inch wide under each of the overlapping boards of the siding. The idea was to give the house an aged look but still be fresh and sturdy.

Behind the main lodge was a smaller structure constructed in the same manner but designed as a storage house for all of the hunting shotguns, rifles, cleaning equipment, ammunition, vests, and other clothing used in the field. In later years, a television was added to the space with comfortable seating to view sports broadcasts. Once, Uncle Walter invited me to do just that. The shrubberies around the buildings were immaculately kept. The front lawn had a featured tree in the center, a great sprawling oak. The tree was so magnificent, with a view of the river from beneath it, that during a time when Charles Lindbergh was a guest, he insisted on pitching a small tent and sleeping under the tree rather than inside! A few yards further out from the tree toward the river, the ground sloped downward at a steep angle to a timbered retaining wall at the river's edge. There were steps going down to a small, but very substantial, wharf. I think it was designed to dock any large boats her guests might use to visit her by water. The view from the top of that manicured bluff was gorgeous. I was invited to a Fourth of July fireworks party hosted by Mrs. Guggenheim to watch fireworks explode all over the night sky above the river one year. I was probably around thirteen at the time. When I was fourteen, she invited me to join a dove hunt she had organized on her property for her guests. Again, like everything done there, the planning was meticulous but appeared effortless.

One other time I met her was when I was much younger, perhaps ten years old. Mrs. Guggenheim and our family were gathered in the caretaker's house my uncle and his family lived in, subsequent to living in the smaller cottage as before. We were all there for an Easter egg hunt planned for that afternoon. It began raining, which cancelled the hunt. So, it was decided that we would spend the rainy time entertaining ourselves in a downstairs family room that was rather large. Along with me, there were several kids assembled for the hunt, including my uncle's two children, brother Lowry, and some other cousins. We spent a good deal of time that afternoon doing what kids do, which is to show off for the adults with our acrobatic skills—somersaults, handstands, and bodily contortions that only limber little bodies can manage—and singing familiar songs. The impressive fact was that Mrs. Guggenheim applauded each "act" and was genuinely smiling the whole afternoon. That was quite an experience for me. There is a book written about her, *The Huntress*. The book is interesting, but I can't speak with any authority on the contents. What I know is based on the very few interactions I had with her and those were extremely positive. She was friendly and outgoing to us and showed an honest interest in what we were doing. I think she was a great person.

My impressions of those times on the Guggenheim property stuck with me. In retrospect, there were several dynamics involved. One, her exposure to great architecture, fine art, and a sense of how to put all that knowledge together so appropriately in a rustic, wooded river setting was evident by her creation of a beautiful retreat on the St. Marys River. Two, she had the financial resources to accomplish her vision. Three, she was there to guide those she retained to accomplish what she ultimately wanted. Four, during her lifetime, she required that everything be maintained in meticulous detail as the years passed.

I was always in awe but, as a young person, I didn't understand the time, cost, and vision it takes to achieve and maintain a dream place like hers. When she passed away in 1963, the guiding light for that wonderful place was extinguished. The river was the same. But the environment she had created on its bank began to fade without her guidance. When I visit that area now, I have memories of what was, and those memories are exceptional. But the reality of what has happened in that environment without her guidance makes me sad. It has slowly sunk into the average state of what is all around it. Only a weak resemblance remains of what it once was. What I've learned by these experiences is that when you can create something special in your life, it is up to you to maintain that specialness. Maintenance is needed for both the physical aspects of a place as well as the spirit of a place. Everything special requires maintenance to keep it so. Specialness can be created. However, without maintenance it will slowly drift down to average or even less. This observation pertains to more in life than simply buildings and grounds. It applies to special human relationships as well.

These three "scenes" in my life illustrate how extraordinary experiences have a profound effect on shaping a personal view of the world. In my earliest years, my experiences were in safe, comfortable environments. That is what I knew. Then, in later years, I was exposed to people and places quite different from what I was familiar with. Did that exposure cause me to think any less of the people and culture I had grown up with? Not at all. I place extremely high value on those early experiences. But these later, new experiences served to expand my comprehension of the world and its possibilities. As my life became more varied with the passage of time, I had more to think about. I added material to be compared and contrasted to the material already in my memory banks. In my examples, the new did not take anything away from the old but instead added new possibilities in my thinking about where life could take me.

ORDER VERSUS CREATIVITY

COLORING BOOKS ARE AN EARLY EXPERIENCE that most young people go through pitting discipline and order against creativity. In the first encounter with this activity, children color everywhere, including encroaching over the lines of the drawing. Once the basic concepts of applying crayons to the drawings and using imagination to choose the colors are set, kids are taught to keep their coloring within the lines provided. Praise accompanies learning to stay within the lines and withheld—maybe even accompanied by an adult's frown—when the coloring is outside of the lines. Staying within the lines instills a sense of correctness and order in the young artists.

In addition to learning discipline with coloring, there are lots of games children learn to play. Most have boundaries that must be observed, much like the coloring lines they were taught to stay within. In the simple game of hopscotch, a grid is drawn on the sidewalk or ground. If a line is stepped on as the player hops through the grid, then their turn is over! In a footrace on an oval track with lanes, stepping over the line into another lane is a disqualifying event. In swimming competitions, straying outside an assigned swim lane results in disqualification. This is the indoctrination into thinking of life's various boundaries and limits. Children who try to get around rules by cheating or lying are scolded, further instilling the need to adhere to proscribed boundaries.

When you become an adult, and coloring books and children's games are left behind, you are still expected to "color within the lines" in ever new and more complex boundaries facing you in everyday life. Some of the boundaries are clear while others are subject to interpretation. For instance, streets and roads have painted lines that come with driving laws you must abide by. Checkout lanes are designated in stores where you shop. These restrictions are simple and clear. Then, there are some boundaries set in law that are fairly straightforward, while other perceived infractions end up in court with judges or juries deciding whether, and to what extent, a boundary was illegally crossed. Organized religions set rules, or boundaries, for their believers to follow. As with the law, some of these rules are straightforward and others not so much. You are inundated with rules, regulations, and boundaries to guide your life. The coloring book was only the beginning. All of this is necessary to prevent chaos in society, and I understand and support such practices. However, I am mindful that living in the world of rules can stifle creative thinking. Stifle, yes, but it does not prevent it. You need creative thinking to improve your life and to adapt to changes in your social and physical environments. This means you need to encourage creative thinking concurrent with teaching and understanding the importance of boundaries. You can accept that rules and boundaries are necessary but remember they are there to control aberrant behavior. Existing rules should not paralyze your creative thinking as you face new or changing circumstances.

History has shown that laws and boundaries are useful and necessary to allow for a civil society that is absent of an intolerable level of chaos. But what will you do when you find yourself in a situation where you believe the right thing to do involves breaking the law or a religious taboo? After you leave your childhood innocence behind and enter the world of adult reality, conflicts will occur between what you sincerely believe is an action you must take and what you suspect or know will bring you afoul of a law. A simple example is a situation where you must transport a person in a critical situation to a hospital because you are not in a position to wait for an ambulance to provide transport. You decide to drive the patient yourself. The time you spend driving is a critical factor in their survival. Will you "break the law" by exceeding the speed limit? Probably so. In a work situation, if you are aware of an imminent life safety situation, will you break a rule or violate a law to rectify the situation before someone is injured or killed? I hope so, even if you might be sanctioned for your action because you "colored outside of the lines." These are only a few examples of the decisions you might face that go against years of conditioning to conform—conditioning that began in early childhood.

The current consternation over illegal immigration is a bigger dilemma. Laws are in place restricting immigration to the limits of certain processes, procedures, and quotas. People around the world are experiencing problems from genocide to rising sea levels forcing them to permanently uproot their lives and leave their home country. Each country potentially receiving these migrating populations has created laws that restrict the number of immigrants it believes it can reasonably absorb. Those limits often are too restrictive to accommodate the vast number of people who desperately need to relocate. As a result, illegal border crossings by desperate people attempting to go from their place of origin to another in order to survive have become daily occurrences. Should these people perish simply to stay within the current rules? They are coloring outside the lines to survive. Shouldn't we find creative solutions to accommodate the ebb and flow of population, from one part of the world to another, without overwhelming the resources of the receiving states? This is a tough situation with life and death consequences.

Governing bodies wrestle with this problem but, to date, have only arrived at temporary solutions, most of which are unacceptable to the populations of the receiving countries. This is an example of one of the tougher boundary situations faced by humanity. The issues involved are complex and vary from one part of the world to another and are further complicated by the receiving countries' biases against given political, economic, and religious views of the affected populations seeking entry. There is a competing need to color outside the lines and a need to honor boundaries. This reinforces the notion that boundaries need to be respected but, at the same time, some boundaries create untenable conditions for society at large and may need to change. Or perhaps the boundaries and the rules regarding boundary enforcement do not need to change if solutions can be found to mitigate the pressure to violate the existing boundaries. This requires creative thinking to achieve practical, workable solutions.

One partial solution that is being pursued is to examine the causes of migration from one country to another. Several of the extreme causes are because of lives disrupted by war, by persistent gang violence, or severe downturns in a country's economic prosperity, leading to job losses with little to no hope of recovery in the near future. Addressing these types of issues can only be affected in a meaningful way by the intervention of a more prosperous country, helping the local country make meaningful changes. It can be done. The obstacles to offering the help are largely caused by lack of popular support. This lack is attributable to little sympathy for the needy country citizens on the part of the more prosperous country. This ambivalence or opposition to offering meaningful help traces to cultural differences and an aversion to diverting a portion of the government budget to another country. For a government to commit to helping another country in ways that are meaningful, a robust communication strategy must be put in place to show citizens in the contributing country how and why it is in their best interests to do so. This is not done well in most cases, but an exception occurred during the Ukrainian war with Russia. The public messaging explained the danger to a free way of life outside of Ukraine and proved powerful in showing what the value of support to Ukraine means for other free countries.

Rising sea levels are a threat to millions of people living on coastal areas that are predicted to be inundated now and decades into the future. The planning for this eventuality must be put into place quickly so that implementation that will take decades to accomplish can be started now. Other than the areas that are already experiencing the effects of sea level rise, most of the world is ignoring the threat that has enormous implications for massive population migrations with astronomical costs. This is another need for a serious and continuous messaging strategy that can best, if not only, be sponsored by national governments. This messaging is embedded in the content of the warnings about the effect of climate change—a warning that is clear but, for multiple reasons, some political, others because the effects are not obvious to the average person in their daily lives, it is not being heeded in a way sufficient to mount a global response that is of the magnitude necessary to offset the changes.

How will these global challenges be met? To be successful, meeting the challenges will require a solid understanding of the details of those challenges, a sound strategic plan, and public messaging of the seriousness and consequences of inaction. The messaging will need to be crafted to overcome cultural and socioeconomic differences. Care will need to be taken to not allow the problems at hand to become politicized, as so many issues do. The messaging will need to be appealing to a majority of the citizenry of each country to be ultimately effective. This means the messaging should be initiated and supported by multi-country organizations, such as the United Nations, the European Union, the World Trade Organization, and other intergovernmental forums.

As with so many other problems that humans face, painful solutions to societal problems are deferred to the future, with hopes that some magical solution will appear, and the problem will go away. This rarely happens. Society accepts their leaders and allows them to stay in power if they are perceived to be acting in societies' best interest. The problem is "best interest" is in the context of the here and now, not some future time. That incentivizes leaders to avoid decisions that bring immediate pain to their followers, even if the decision is in society's long-term best interest. In the problem of immigration, many of the future pressures to make large-scale migrations are known today. But to implement plans that will circumvent or alleviate those pressures would cause pain. So, the "can is kicked down the road" to not cause society's current leaders to fall into disfavor. A glaring example is knowing that sea levels are on the rise, and with that, huge percentages of the world's population living in low lying areas will be forced to migrate as their lands are submerged under the sea.

Logically, the world's leadership should be orchestrating an orderly movement out of these areas in the time there is left. But, no, that will be costly and unpopular, so logical decisions will be delayed until there is no choice but to move people as the land is inundated, and a crisis is created so the leadership can say they are *forced* to act, saying they know this is unpopular but what choice do they have? I'm opposed to having politicians elected for life to remove some of the incentive for executing plans in the present for rewards that come decades later.

As an alternative to bowing to short-term pressures to keep the status quo, a study group at the national level should be created. They would develop strategies for heading off future calamities that don't take a genius to predict and have congressional authority to implement tactical measures in the here and now envisioned in the long-term strategy. Congress could approve an annual budget for the group's use and thereby create distance from the political fallout to some degree. There are agencies currently within the government that have semi-autonomy, such as the National Security Agency (NSA) and the Central Intelligence Agency (CIA). These agencies have congressional oversight, but their activities are not reported on a regular basis in the daily news cycle. The downside to this recommendation is that the public will not be timely informed of their activities. The upside is that without the group's activities reported on a daily basis, those activities lose their appeal for politicization. A twist in this is that the leaders of these organizations are "appointed" to their positions and that process is subject to political bias. Being that this country is a constitutional republic, I don't have an alternative to offer in that process. Even approval of the appointments by Congress does not remove the potential for bias.

In laying the groundwork for creative leadership in the future, teachers need to encourage creative thinking in students concurrent with teaching them about boundaries. Students eventually become a continuation of the leadership needed to solve the seemingly intractable problems that humanity is, and will be, confronted with. A key to success in creating the next generation of positive leaders depends upon the quality of the administration and teachers in the education system, including the school board and the principals they have chosen to lead each school. The principals will be instrumental in the selection and retention of the teachers or faculty. The school board is typically an elected body. For a school system that gives the youth of a community their best shot at success, the community-at-large must understand what is at stake and choose their board members wisely. This whole system is under the auspices of the relevant local and state governments.

Finally, *we the people*, are the ones who elect our national leaders based on our personal decisions when we vote. We collectively have enormous input into the choice of our national leaders, their integrity, their wisdom, and their philosophy of governance. Finally, what we get, right down to the quality and effectiveness of our school systems, is up to the nation's citizens and the individuals chosen by those same citizens to lead the country. It is too easy and too simple to put blame on a political party for any grievances. They were put in power at the ballot box—so it is imperative that voters know the character and capabilities of every candidate for office and what they stand for. It is imperative that we get our choices right, based on logic and reason, not on choices based on emotionally charged political messaging. Only then will we get the creative leaders we need to solve our national problems while, at the same time, preserving stability in our lives through maintenance of discipline and order. A climate of discipline and order does not necessarily exclude creativity. They can be achieved together. They are not mutually exclusive.

I was once an observer in an engineering class at Arizona State University. I came into the class after a practical exercise had begun. The professor shared with me the instructions he had given the class, which had been divided into about eight competing teams. Each team had been given a large stack of newsprint and given the objective to be the first team to use that material to touch the ceiling of the classroom within a specific time limit. The teams had started the competition before I had arrived and were busy rolling the newsprint into rigid tubes and using the tubes to construct elaborate towers to reach the ceiling. It was slow going and it didn't look like any team would touch the ceiling before the allotted time expired. Finally, desperate, one student asked the professor if it would be permissible to simply stand on one of the worktables and hold one of the rolled tubes as high as needed to touch the ceiling. The professor answered, "Sure, the instruction was to figure out how to touch the ceiling with the paper."

There were a lot of dynamics at work here with the competing teams. They hadn't taken the time to thoughtfully parse out the words in the instruction as what to do. The specific time limit seemed to suggest that the solution to the problem would take the entire time. When one team sprang into action to build a tower, beginning on the floor and working up, creativity ceased as the other teams assumed a tower was the solution. The challenge soon became a race to design and build a tower to the ceiling faster than the other teams. Boundaries, or coloring inside the lines, seemed to dominate their thinking. This exercise exposed thinking limited by presumptions about what the boundary conditions were and taking the first idea of a solution to a problem as the solution without further creative thought. Succumbing to the pressure of getting started on *something*, so as not to fall behind the team who had jumped off to a fast start was evident in the frenzied activity of the other teams. Allowing the pressure of a time limit, a red herring in this case, to generate quick action before thinking through the problem to be solved was another reaction. The fact that each team was given a large stack of newsprint implied that all of it was needed to achieve the objective. I was impressed by how much there was to learn crammed into that simple exercise.

There is a need to keep the spark of creativity alive in children living in our world of rules. Reacting to this need, some organizations have offered schooling that is less structured and more free form than traditional public schooling. I'm not an advocate of that non-traditional approach as a stand-alone philosophy, simply because in a world of rules and laws, kids need to be conditioned to expect that restrictions and consequences will be encountered in life. However, I do believe that within public schools, there should be exercises in non-traditional approaches to problem-solving woven into the curriculum. In addition, while parents or other adults in a child's life help them to develop a sense of personal responsibility, a sense of right versus wrong, and the development of a strong moral code, teachers should also be imparting the knowledge that the child will eventually be faced with decisions requiring coloring outside the lines as a moral imperative as they mature. This early assistance in developing these characteristics will prepare them to make decisions they believe are right, understand the potential consequences, and be prepared to face society's judgment of the outcome.

There are scores of public figures who color outside the lines. Unfortunately, these public figures sometimes engage in this behavior only to get attention and regular mention in the media. If their behavior is successful, even though it is without any moral grounding, it will lead many in the public to see their success and emulate their actions in their own lives. When I learn of these situations where public figures flaunt the rules simply to say, "look at me!" I can see such behavior can be traced back to the adult influences in their childhood.

⁓⁄⁞⁖⁓

Politics and Governments

DECISIONS AND MISTAKES

I AM ENTHRALLED EACH NEW YEAR by the unveiling of the latest, greatest advances in the automobile industry. The marketing strategy involves a responsible adult-like listing of the latest safety technology. Then, the sales pitch shifts to what really sells: more speed and power than was available in last year's models. An additional sweetener is the revelation of a bigger and more robust "infotainment" center with an enhanced sound system that has speakers powerful enough to serve a football stadium. Men, although not exclusively, are drawn to the number of seconds to speed from 0 to 60 miles per hour; the fewer seconds under six, the more exciting and the top speed must reach at least 135 miles per hour. These features are considered "must haves" by many. I mean, you never know when it will be necessary to make an emergency run to the grocery store for beer or crackers. What is missing in the new, faster, and more powerful machines is a driver with the maturity and adequate reflexes to control the unexpected situations—the new, faster cars now offer far less reaction time for the driver to avoid disaster. My possibly exaggerated point is that our scientists, engineers, and others involved in the creative process offering new products and services to the public sometimes introduce products that exceed the public's capacity to absorb and control the advances offered.

In a more serious vein, the advent of atomic power, useful in energy generation, was also the beginning of increasingly horrific means of mass destruction in the form of nuclear weapons. These weapons are increasingly available to nation after nation, some of which are led by despots teetering on the edge of insanity. The information available on the internet to anyone old enough to manipulate a keyboard is unbelievable in scope and content. By one measure, the internet is a boon to the world and an accelerant to gaining more knowledge about anything desired. By another measure, the technology allowed various social media platforms to be created that are sometimes used for bullying, rapid dissemination of misinformation, destruction of reputations, and access to the "dark web"—online portals for finding services and products outlawed in the civilized world. I'm reminded of the answer to the age-old question, "Why do you do it?" with the answer being, "Because I can."

This ability of humanity to produce products and services that exceed the mental, emotional, and ethical grasp of many who partake of them is a serious problem. Every high school, college, and university should include serious discussions of the potential harmful uses of new technologies and feats of engineering. These discussions should raise awareness in the creative minds of the next generation of superstars of their responsibilities. These responsibilities include thinking through the potential uses, good and bad, of their fledgling ideas before moving forward with full development of their innovations. Moral and ethical considerations should be guiding forces. Finally, if a bold innovation is born, these same ethical and moral standards should be applied to marketing strategies. I'm all for creativity, innovation, and a "wow" factor in what will be available to me in the future. But I know what is available to me will be available to everyone, no matter their level of personal responsibility or maturity. My hope is that the creators of marvelous new things will take every precaution they can envision in their development to prevent an unintended release of a harmful or destructive product.

As the plastics technology evolved, it was heralded as a modern miracle improving our everyday lives in many ways. Foods are wrapped in it to preserve freshness, inexpensive plastic bags are available to transport purchases from store to home, bottles are made from it to hold our beverages, and other uses too numerous to mention. But as the proliferation of plastics has continued with increasing volume, the plastic substances are accumulating in the environment at a staggering rate, a proliferation certainly not anticipated by the early developers of this now ubiquitous substance.

Microplastics, fragments of the plastics used to create drinking cups, bottles, fishing nets, ropes, and the like have now entered the food stream consumed by humans as well as in the air. How the human body will adapt to this new element infusing our bodies is still to be determined. Now that we are aware of these serious problems with this truly useful material, there are efforts underway to manage the problem, as it currently exists. However, as management efforts begin to take hold, will they be offset by innovative *new* uses of plastics that will offset the drive to curtail the current problems?

The answer is yes, they will, unless the innovators who choose to work with plastics begin to see their creations in an environmentally holistic way, creating in their planned products offsets such that they do not add to the plastic problems. An example could be designing certain plastics to contain an enzyme that would degrade the plastic to a benign substance in a reasonable time consistent with the desired lifetime of the product. A disposable plastic drinking cup needs to last for a time in an inventory prior to retail sale, hold up through the intended use by the consumer, and the time for transport to a landfill. This would suggest being designed for a life of approximately three years. It is common practice to label food containers with a "best by" date or some other designation of expiration. It would not be difficult to label plastic products with a designed expiration in a similar fashion.

The development of robots to handle human tasks is not new. Robotics are commonplace in automobile and manufacturing assembly lines. Military and police use small, boxlike mobile robots to examine, analyze, and even detonate objects suspected of being explosives. There is a fascination in popular science fiction with robots becoming sentient beings, aware of their surroundings and making decisions without human guidance. Creative people are curious to see if they can develop a robot with human-like, physical characteristics that are capable of feeling emotions and making independent decisions based on reactions to the environment around them. Will this development also include moral and ethical grounding in the robot's decisions and actions? This is difficult enough to achieve in humans! So, what would it take to instill these traits in a human-like machine? If even possible, the standards for ethical and moral values used in the robot's development would be subject to the value systems of its human creators.

I am all for pushing forward with new ideas and new ways to improve the human condition. However, questions should be asked and answered with a view to anticipate trouble down the road to offset potential troubles. The disparity between the essential creativity needed to improve the lot of humanity and the irresponsible use of the results of that creativity among some in the population has always been around. That disparity needs to be recognized in educational systems that teach budding engineers, chemists, and those in the sciences to be aware of the potential misuse of their advances in creating new ways of living for the masses. Once a newly invented genie is out of the bottle, it is out. With every year that passes, I believe humanity is becoming more aware of the necessity to avoid the mistakes of the past that have harmed our environment and, by extension, humanity. Some steps are being taken to mitigate these mistakes and prevent new problems in the future. Ozone-layer-depleting freon has been banned, DDT was taken off the market for pesticide use, asbestos is no longer used in building materials, and lead paints are banned. Progress is being made.

STORIES OF WAR

ONE OF THE VERY FEW WAR stories Grandfather Keefe told me was about his time in France during World War I. His story had an influence on me when I became an officer. He was an army engineer working on the French battlefields, restoring war-damaged rail lines used to support the troops. He described a situation in a combat zone when he and some other weary soldiers returned to their base camp for the night. When they arrived, they were informed they had a new captain assigned as their leader who was fresh from the United States. The captain's first action with his new command was to have them form up in ranks for his inspection. One exhausted soldier, having just returned from the fighting on the front, was singled out for abuse over the fact he was missing a button on his tunic. That night, while camped in a combat zone, the captain had the troops give up their weapons to stack them outside their respective tents, much as they may have done in training situations in the United States during peacetime. The consensus his order generated among the battle-hardened soldiers was that this captain was going to get them killed. The next day, they returned to the fighting in the trenches. As this first day under the new command passed and the fighting subsided, the captain was found dead, with dozens of bullet wounds in his back. I know when my time as an officer in the military came, this story I heard in my childhood had a meaningful influence in my interactions with those I was chosen to lead.

After the event with the captain, Grandfather Keefe was wounded by shrapnel from an exploding artillery shell, which upended the small railway repair vehicle he was riding on, throwing him to the ground off the tracks. He survived by hiding, for a time, under some nearby shrubs as German Army soldiers moved through the area. He was later found by Allied troops and sent to a military field hospital for his wounded leg. He recalled lying in the field hospital tent with three doctors standing over him. Two of the doctors were saying the damage to his leg was so bad it needed to be amputated. The third doctor, younger than the other two, thought the leg could be saved. Grandfather then passed out. When he awoke sometime later, he looked down and, with great relief, saw that the younger doctor had obviously convinced the others his leg could be saved because it was still there. He was then transported to a hospital in England for recovery. While there, a couple of nurses took him boating on a lake adjacent to the hospital. One of the nurses who couldn't swim fell overboard. Grandfather jumped out of the boat with his injured leg in a cast, grabbed the nurse, and managed to get her back to the boat. The other nurse pulled them back into the boat. He was hailed as a hero when they returned to the hospital. But it was wartime, so he was soon sent back to the front, using a cane for support, and assigned to a field ambulance. He was wounded again and returned to the States. I have a picture of a very nice-looking young English woman from that time. Aunt Gerri tells me she was named Marjorie, who was his girlfriend before he met my grandmother. I wonder if she was the nurse he pulled from the lake. I'll never know but I have my suspicions!

Writing about Grandfather's wartime experience leads me to another breadcrumb on the trail of finding my philosophy of life. My father was in World War II and traveled to Europe on the Queen Mary, which had been converted from civilian use to a military transport ship. He said there were stormy seas on the way over, which had many of the troops spending their time throwing up. When they arrived in Belgium, it was winter with heavy snow. As a rifleman in the infantry, he told me they basically walked all the way across Belgium, fighting German soldiers most of the way. He received several battlefield promotions as those above him were killed. He started as a private and moved up in rank through those battlefield promotions to the position of a staff sergeant.

One of the stories Dad told coming out of the long trek across Belgium is like my Grandfather Keefe's story about the poor leadership of the captain in World War I. This story may have affected me as well. He recounted how his squad was moving through a village occupied by German troops. Dad said that during the fighting, his lieutenant ordered him, a sergeant, to move his squad from a spot behind a building across an open area to the cover of a house beyond. He told the lieutenant that move was a bad idea, since an enemy machine gun emplacement covered the open area. The inexperienced lieutenant insisted. Not willing to risk the lives of his men, Dad stripped off his field gear and, with a running start, dashed from cover, across the open area, and turned and raced back—all while enemy machine gun bullets were whipping through the air around him. The shocked lieutenant agreed then that having his men attempt to cross the area was a bad idea. Maybe that was one of those lessons that stuck with me when I was an officer: the advice of seasoned non-coms was something I should listen to. Further, when in post-military leadership positions, I listened carefully to the advice given by seasoned supervisors. Not that I always followed their advice, but I certainly gave serious consideration to what they had to say.

The last part of his journey across Belgium was in the Ardennes Forest, the heavily wooded area the Allies never expected the Germans to use as an avenue of attack. Well, that proved wrong, and it was a major front in the Battle of the Bulge. Dad was injured in that encounter when an enemy shell exploded on the front of a battle tank he had hitched a ride on. Due to the injury, he was sent back from the front to a job in an army finance company for the duration. I learned many years later that my father-in-law, who was in the 101st Airborne Division, was one of those fighting in Bastogne at the time, about twenty miles from my father. It's a small world. My wife and I have visited Bastogne and the military museum there. I certainly recommend it to anyone having the opportunity to do so. I also had the chance a few years ago to tour the Queen Mary, which is docked in Long Beach, California as a museum, outfitted with bunk beds and other equipment that supported its use as a troop transport during the war.

I was also told a story about an instance in the Battle of the Bulge by a man who worked for me at Madison College, who I'll call Hal. This is not a story of heroism, and there is no braggadocio involved; it's just a reaction to mind-numbing combat during an encounter that lasted only a few seconds. Hal and I were talking about our relative experiences in military basic training, even though our service stints were about twenty-five years apart. I was describing the bayonet training we received, getting into the detailed techniques of how to parry and thrust and so forth, and then asked if he ever had to use any of that complex training in his combat experience. He looked at me and explained that in the fighting he was in, with all the chaotic screaming, gunfire, and explosions, he was just trying to get out alive. In response to the use of his bayonet training, his one bayonet encounter went something like this. Hal was not a tall guy, maybe around five-foot-five-inches, when a much larger German soldier in the assault force came charging at him head on. I got the impression that both were terrified and fighting on instinct rather than calculated combat moves. Hal said as he saw his imminent collision with the enemy, he lowered his head, closed his eyes, and leaned forward, holding his rifle with the bayonet in front of his body. To his amazement, the big German soldier ran straight into his bayonet and impaled himself. That was it. I sensed Hal was still somewhat in amazement, all those years later, that he survived the war.

This story is a reminder of how life can either end or survive in the flash of a single action. In an instant, the German soldier died, and the American soldier lived. Both were serving their respective countries and neither wanted to die. But, in war, people live and people die. For those who die young, the short time on earth experiencing the miracle of life is truncated. That is a tragedy of war. In the Bible, Matthew 24:6 says, "And ye shall hear of wars and rumors of wars: see that you are not troubled: for all these things must come to pass, but the end is not yet." While this verse is meant to comfort, it is recognition in a religious text of the permanence of war. I served in the United States military and am proud of that service and would do it again if called to protect my country and freedom. But I have no illusions about the horror of it all. I am an advocate of having a strong national military, as I firmly believe it is a deterrent to war rather than the other way around. But if deterrence fails, I want to prevail in any subsequent war. I respect the precious nature of life. Ending a life in a combat situation is nothing short of a tragic waste of life. However, sometimes the alternative to war is to lose one's freedom, or worse. So, a nation as a collective body makes a decision, weighing the fact that lives will be lost against the fate of being subjugated to another nation. This is a terrible decision to be faced with, but this is the reality of the world we live and die in.

One of the ironies of war is how once bitter enemies can later become friends and allies. With the movement of people around the world, natives of one land having moved to another become combatants against their ancestral country. For example, my father was born in this country, as was his father. Their ancestors came here from Germany. My grandfather fought with the United States Army against the Germans in World War I, and my father fought against the Germans in World War II. When my time in the military came, I was stationed in Germany, which by that time had become an ally of the United States during the Cold War with the common enemy being Russia. Later, I married Ksenia, who was born in the United States of parents who were also born here but whose ancestry was Russian and Ukrainian.

As night would begin to fall on my grandparents' house in Jamestown, and when Dad would come home from work, my family would often sit out on the grassy side yard of the house in some very comfortable lawn chairs. At least the adults did; I think I sat in the grass with my dog, a big German Shepard I named Dance. Present would be Grandfather, Grandmother, Mother, Dad, and me. Sometimes my aunt and uncle would join us. The adults would tell stories about life. Grandfather was probably the best at storytelling. His stories always seemed to have a moral to them. I know I soaked all of that up. Rarely, the stories would be about their time in the military. All my adult male relatives were in the wars. The stories were about their experiences to the extent they talked about them. There was a strong reluctance among their generations to talk about what had happened and they were no exception. What I did get from the limited number of times they did talk about their war experiences was that they were not sorry they served. Their experiences were horrific, but they did what they needed to do and survived—unlike many of their comrades. What I seemed to absorb was that if I was ever called to serve, I would do my best like they did. Their few stories were quite extraordinary. They were fortunate to have lived through their wartime service, but I do not ever remember them glorifying war or acting as if anything was heroic about it, even though there were certainly heroes among them. This was something they just believed must be done in times of threat to our nation.

The impression of service to country stuck with me as I reached my twenties. The war in Vietnam was happening at that time, and the military draft was in effect. I was just finishing a master's degree in college when I received my draft notice. I knew people in my age group who were already in the Vietnam War: some had served and returned, some were still there, and others had been killed or missing in action. There was a great deal of discussion among my peers as to how they would respond when their draft notice arrived. There had been different avenues for deferment during the years of the war, one of which was being a conscientious objector. One person I knew very well availed himself of that route, claiming a religious affiliation of which I was totally unaware. Others discussed moving to Canada, some concocted plans to fake some sort of physical disability and, in one case, I had a guy describe to me how if he turned his head a certain way, he could pick up a local radio station. He told me he was anxious to explain that when his time came to be examined during his draft physical in hopes of being classified unfit to serve. I wish I knew how that plan turned out, but I have doubts about its success.

Another interesting ploy was the idea that if you held a bar of a certain brand of soap under your armpit the night before your physical, it would cause your blood pressure to be elevated to a level that would cause you to fail the test. I never heard of anyone succeeding with that scheme. I thought about the idea of moving to Canada, which was an idea that several young men I knew brought up. It took me about three seconds to decide that was a bad idea. I believe my childhood affiliation with relatives who had all served influenced me to never seriously consider any route other than to comply with the draft notice. Once that was clear in my head, I decided that if that were my future, I would prefer to serve as an officer. With that in mind, I proceeded to the induction center in Atlanta, where I was living at the time, to join the army, rather than report for induction the next day in my hometown of Waycross many miles away. I stated my preference to become an officer and learned the process was for me to go through basic training, advanced individual training, and then attend Officer Candidate School. I did those things and was commissioned a Second Lieutenant in the United States Army. After a few more short training commitments, I was assigned to a unit in Germany for two years.

The military experience was very rewarding in several ways. My exposure to many people from all levels of society was extraordinary. Despite some of the criticisms of unfairness in how the draft was administered, it still generated a pool of soldiers that was a true mixture of the diversity of the country—and I was in the middle of that. It was a personal growth experience that would have been impossible for me to have in any other way. Then, to be sent to Europe, specifically Germany, to live for two years was another experience I know I would not have been able to replicate other than being in the army. It was a matter of timing that put me in Germany rather than Vietnam. When my class graduated from Officer Candidate School, the war there was starting to wind down and, at that time, the army didn't need a new batch of second lieutenants with our particular training in Vietnam. So, they sent us to other assignments, and I went to Germany. During the two years of that assignment, I took advantage of the opportunity to travel all around Europe during times when I had leave. That travel exposed me to parts of the world that were unlike what I had experienced before. For years after I was no longer in the military, I had a number of opportunities—created through my working career and during personal vacation times—to visit countries in Europe. My earlier experiences living there fostered a strong desire to seek opportunities for return visits. This new and exciting part of my life was a direct result of my openness to serve in the military when I was called.

The stories I heard from my parents, grandparents, and uncles who had all served conditioned me to accept this call to service as simply a part of my life. I think their stories also led me to believe that if I became an officer, I might have a little more control over my life in the military than otherwise. This turned out to be very true, so the added time commitment required to become an officer was not troubling to me. I credit this positive life experience to my family's influence on me as a child regarding military service. While I probably would not have volunteered for the military during the war with Vietnam, my attitude when I was selected to serve was not one of dread or a desire to find a way out. That attitude contributed to my choice to pursue being an officer to make the best of the situation. In retrospect, my time in the military was a most rewarding experience and contributed enormously to my personal growth as a human being. This time gave me an enormous respect for the power the United States military can bring to bear when called upon to protect our country and the professional way that obligation is managed.

The military leaders I was exposed to saw war as a terrible thing that should be avoided but, when called upon to protect the nation, the United States military is a fearsome power to be reckoned with by our adversaries. To put it simply, there are nations in the world with malevolent leaders with expansionist ambitions. History is replete with examples of weak nations being preyed upon by stronger nations. The United States must stay strong in order not to become one of those preyed upon and be willing to use force if confronted. This does not mean I condone war—far from it. But if my country is attacked, I will support going to war to protect it. Threats to the United States can build on the other side of the world with just a matter of time until the threat is a direct one. Therefore, I support being a part of the North Atlantic Treaty Organization (NATO) and further support Article 5 of the charter that pledges our military support if any NATO member is attacked.

When war does become inevitable, I view it as one of the tragedies of human life. War has been a constant through human history, with some regions of the world enjoying relative peace for a time but are ultimately drawn back into conflict and war. I recognize that threats to this country will continue. There will be breaks in the severity of the threats but, make no mistake, the threats are there and can balloon into full-blown conflict at any time. The country's leadership and populace should not allow peacetime complacence to set in between periods of extreme conflict and allow the effectiveness of the military to decline. Weakness in this area will only invite aggression from foreign actors. Care should always be taken to keep alliances with key partners strong, as there will be a time of mutual need. In times of relative peace, competition is strong to divert federal funding of the nation's military budget to other perceived needs, particularly those with strong appeal to voters during election seasons. But these diversions are serious mistakes and put our nation at grave risk.

STRONG OPINIONS

WHILE DISCUSSING CONTROVERSIAL POSITIONS THAT DEAL with subjects such as life and death, there are a lot of nuances in what a person says they value. I find this true about my values when I think through controversial issues and stake out a position representing my thoughts and feelings. I believe that life as a human being is a miracle. To be on this planet at this time in infinity where environmental conditions allow life to exist as we know it speaks to the impossible odds that human life would occur at all. And, when this miracle does occur, the resulting life is very short in the grand scheme of things. Taking an action to shorten or terminate a life is a weird phenomenon that humans seem to do too often. The seriousness of such an action and its consequences are addressed in many religious doctrines and embedded in secular law.

When confronting life-or-death decisions, humans have an ability to rationalize and compartmentalize events, allowing for a life of relative sanity. Most humans develop a sense of right and wrong, a sense of grief for lost loved ones, a love for others, and a sense of guilt for actions they are ashamed of. Any of these senses can be overwhelming at times but, fortunately, the uncomfortable ones can be shut out over time through compartmentalization or rationalization. These protections are not absolute, in that the shut-away feelings come back from time to time. For most people, such feelings don't come back to the point of debilitation or, at the extreme, insanity.

These abilities to compartmentalize or rationalize are in play when a person is involved in a decision regarding ending a life. I'm glad these emotional circuit breakers are in the human psyche to help cope with the aftermath of such a decision. They may not work to perfection, as demonstrated by the common experience of post-traumatic stress disorder, or PTSD, suffered by so many military veterans and police officers. But they are there. The downside of this protective ability is that some rare individuals can use this ability to rationalize life-or-death decisions they make with an almost sociopathic ease. This extreme is certainly not a desirable trait and one that has negative moral and ethical results for society.

There are times in life when decisions must, or in some cases should, be taken that involve ending another's life. These decisions have much in common with what I have said about the conflicts posed by living in a world of rules and order. Sometimes the answers sought in personal decisions involving life and death can't be found in the rules laid out in the secular world meant to guide my actions. There are times when my decisions might result in life-or-death outcomes. In those times, I must reach deep into my inner self to find answers to guide my decisions that I can live with in the aftermath. The emotional circuit breakers I have mentioned are helpful in these times, but they are only that: helpful. They do not preclude the trauma and sometimes gut-wrenching pain that accompanies these decisions.

Situations in which a family member is in a hospital, the prognosis is awful, and the question arises from the medical team for the family as to their decision on removing artificial life support. Military personnel and police officers face life-ending decisions more than most, as their professions require them to make such decisions as part of their jobs. In the abstract, people have strong opinions about what decisions they would make and why they would make them. But when a situation facing a person goes from hypothetical to painfully real, the strong opinions held beforehand start to break down when real-time events are revealing details to be considered that weren't part of the hypothetical discussions. This is when having developed a strong, overarching set of moral, ethical, and empathetic sensibilities becomes the bedrock from which to find the way forward with a decision that involves life and death.

There are two situations that are good examples of decisions that become very difficult when faced in the real world versus discussed in the abstract. These are the decisions surrounding abortion and capital punishment. A person's beliefs and positions on these issues develop over time, since the questions are complicated and viewed through the rational, emotional, religious, and sometimes legal lenses that a person has developed over a lifetime. But will these beliefs and possibly publicly stated positions hold when confronted with a requirement to make a personal decision that will determine a specific outcome? Often I have been asked, or have asked myself, about my position on these two issues. I could choose a bumper sticker answer such as "I believe in the right to life," or "I oppose capital punishment." These are easy answers, but these are not really fulsome answers. These questions deserve examination before compressing their answers into simple statements. And this examination, if taken thoughtfully and seriously by anyone, will reveal more about a person's views on life than the specific questions posed.

Abortion is defined as the deliberate termination of a human pregnancy. As a first reaction to this definition, I might respond with a statement that it should not be done. A life that is conceived is too precious to end before it has a chance outside the womb. Now, my initial, terse response comes from a combination of personal application of a little logic, a lot of emotion, and underlying spiritual values. I don't think I'm unusual in having a first opinion based on those three factors. However, recognizing that these same subjective biases are shared by those in positions of power who create the laws regarding this subject and who embed those biases in the legal framework of those laws is disturbing.

In the founding of this country, there was a desire to have a government that was not beholden to royalty and a desire to be free in how one worshiped without a particular faith being dictated by the government. Elected officials we choose to lead the country come from different religious affiliations, but these are predominantly Judeo-Christian. There are variations in how leadership in the three branches of government interpret the doctrines in the religions of which they profess to be a part. When laws are enacted or interpreted, these leaders, being human, can't always help but to imbue logical thinking with a bias toward their personal, spiritual values. Or, I must cynically say, in some cases toward a spiritual bias that pleases a large portion of their constituency.

Over the years, the addition of personal, spiritual values by politicians to the decision-making process in establishing the laws of the land will slowly erode the separation of church and state, potentially leading to a loss of individual religious freedom. When laws are established governing abortion, the citizens of this country have varying spiritual values, which may or may not be in sync with the values of the political leaders whose spiritual values may bias the laws. Political leaders should curb the desire to include very specific tenets of their particular religion as they engage in crafting legislation. Government intrusion into religious affairs, even if well intended, will erode citizens' ability to worship as they choose, which I strongly believe is a strength of the United States.

Wouldn't it be good to have rational laws meant to protect an unborn life but that also allow room for individual, spiritual beliefs to have weight in one of life's most difficult decisions? Laws should leave room for a parents' spiritual values to be considered, not taken away. Still, there are considerations in addition to religious ones that need to be taken into account. Simplistic pronouncements made in the public debate on how laws should be written to govern abortion do not always recognize the realities that some will face unwanted pregnancies. The origins are varied, sometimes extreme, and quite deserving of exception to any blanket declaration that abortions should not be performed under any circumstances.

As examples of the extremes on the spectrum of realities, here are a few: pregnancy created through incest; pregnancy of minors; pregnancy of people with physical or intellectual disabilities who have been taken advantage of; rape, under any circumstances, is barbaric and criminal and may be the cause of pregnancy. These instances, some might say, have nothing to do with terminating an innocent life who had nothing to do with those circumstances. I understand that argument and I can see its merits. But the merits do not negate consideration for the expectant mother's life. Isn't that life worth protecting as well? It is to me. I don't mean only through pregnancy and birth but protecting a pregnant person's mental health and future economic viability.

The question as to whether to abort a pregnancy should be considered within the domain of the people closest to the mother and, crucially, with the people they choose to consult with. These could include family or trusted friends, the father, a religious advisor, or a social worker with experience in these matters. I was included as one of those chosen as a confidant by a pregnant woman facing this very emotional decision-making process. It was a deeply moving experience for me in an area I had no preparation for. My task was to search for any information I could find that would result in a reasonably safe abortion without involvement of medical professionals. I had to report that I could not find any. In the end, she decided to marry the father and have the baby. Laws enacted in this arena should allow reasonable time for the mother to avail herself of this support in the decision-making process prior to dealing with the questions of law. In any significant decision I must make, I look at the pros and cons of the choice facing me. In most cases, there is a risk to be considered if I choose poorly. Then, I consider what risk I can live with in the choice I make. This time for thoughtful consideration has always mitigated any remorse I may have later if my ultimate decision leads to an undesirable outcome.

Laws enacted restricting abortion should allow reasonable time for the mother to give thoughtful consideration to the decision and to think through living with that decision later. Laws should also include an appeal process if the desired outcome is contrary to what is enshrined in those laws. Governmental bodies creating laws that satisfy a political calculus without the expectant mother having some specific, legal avenues of appeal in extreme circumstances trouble me. The laws that are enacted should specifically provide for unbiased review boards to hear these cases that conflict with the law, ideally composed of medical professionals, social services professionals, as well as legal advisors. In instances where the determination of the board is *not* to approve termination of the pregnancy, but it is clear the mother will be incapable of raising the child, then the law should provide a social safety net to accommodate the circumstances to the extent reasonable and practical.

Perhaps the safety net could involve collaboration with church or social service agencies that provide adoption services. Each situation should be evaluated on its own merits. Laws in this area should be written with care not to preordain outcomes prior to review and consideration of the individual situations that fall within the eligibility requirements written in the law for consideration by a review board. These review boards must be accessible and capable of timely review. Having these boards fall under the purview of county health departments would be a reasonable way to meet this need. It would also facilitate access to pertinent local records regarding the applicant. If the determination were that an abortion could proceed, that would allow for competent medical personnel to be involved without the specter of being charged with a criminal act.

There are times when an abortion may be the right call when the life of the mother is in danger. Under some state laws, anyone participating or aiding in an abortion are subject to prosecution. This puts doctors in a precarious situation, as they will be aware that their medical opinion that an abortion to save the mother's life is necessary or some other anomaly with the fetus needs to be addressed, may be challenged after the fact with the possible result of losing their license, fines, or even imprisonment. If a review board could be accessed prior to the medical procedure being performed, that would give doctors protection from disputes over their decisions.

I appreciate the need for law in this area, but I do not agree with draconian measures that refuse to allow for or accommodate outliers, of which there are many. There should be protection for an unborn child, but I am firmly on the side of the expectant mother having the opportunity for input into the decision within the restrictions of a legal framework that recognizes that decisions need to take into consideration too many variables to be enumerated in a specific law. So, the law should allow for a means for the variables to be considered. Any laws enacted to limit the mother's options should allow for reasonable review of the individual circumstances in each situation. Make no mistake; I don't condone someone using abortion multiple times in their life as a means of birth control. That is a different situation altogether.

Capital punishment, or the sentencing of a human to death as punishment for a crime, is another subject that deserves more than a bumper sticker response. When asked, "Do you support capital punishment?" based on my view of life, the simple answer is yes, I do support capital punishment. But this is an area that deserves a more robust response. In some parts of the world, capital punishment is meted out for a variety of offenses both for violations of law and for violations of religious taboos. A death sentence for homosexuality, for infidelity, or blasphemous speech is beyond the pale. Means of execution, often meant as a deterrent for similar behavior or as a painfully gruesome way to exact revenge or make a political statement, are also unacceptable. I value the precious nature of a human life, and I do not believe in extinguishing it except in rare circumstances where the person in question has forfeited that life through egregious circumstances.

In the United States, the laws governing capital punishment are very limiting and involve a judge, jury, and adherence to very strict legal boundaries. I don't advocate for laws that completely forbid capital punishment, as there are those who have committed heinous crimes, often with forethought, or those who have a likely predisposition to commit further similar crimes in the future. One prominent example are mass shootings.

In discussing this topic with others, I hear the objection, "What if after twenty years in prison, DNA testing or other new evidence is revealed that leads to the sentence being commuted?" It's a good question. The sentencing guidelines for judges could require that to render a sentence of execution, the evidence in the case must be supported by more than one eyewitness to a murder, not including relatives of the suspect. If video is presented, it must clearly show the face of the suspect in the commission of the crime. If police are involved, the evidence must show conclusive video images of the perpetrator in the act, or that more than two officers were witnesses to the killing. Confessions will not be allowed as evidence to support the death penalty, as those are suspect in too many past convictions. These restrictions, plus those already found in law, should eliminate the possibility of a wrongful sentence of death and instead result in a life sentence if the remaining evidence is deemed supportive of conviction.

However, when a perpetrator is judged to receive a sentence of death, it should be done by a method that is not cruel or needlessly painful. The particular methods currently used are for show; strapping the condemned person in a chair and applying deadly electrical current or injecting chemical concoctions with a bevy of witnesses present. Medical procedures are carried out in this country every day with the patient rendered unconscious and experiencing no pain at all. It would be a small step to prevent reawakening. But in order to maintain the fantasy that anesthesia used for medical procedures is "safe" for patients, our laws prevent the use of painless medications used in everyday medical procedures to be used in fulfilling a death sentence.

As a result, the means used are those that aren't acceptable in a medical procedure. That leaves electricity and chemical concoctions as "humane" alternatives to hanging or firing squads. The point should be to end the life, not torture the perpetrator in some barbaric spectacle. A life sentence spent locked in a small room without the possibility of parole as an alternative to a death sentence falls into the category of barbaric. Even so, there are cases that justify this as an alternative to the death penalty for a judge and jury. I support capital punishment but in limited circumstances, and only when its imposition is carefully considered by a judge, jury, and within limited circumstances delineated in law.

It is important to take time in life to contemplate some of the situations everyone will face at one time or another that will require making decisions involving life and death. You cannot know in advance what your decisions will be but at least you can prepare yourself, to some extent, by taking time periodically to review your values based on your life experiences. These values will, at minimum, provide a framework from which you can work through a course of action in each circumstance—often a circumstance not allowing time for lengthy introspection. This is why I used the topics of abortion and capital punishment to show how some of our thoughts on issues of importance may not be as clear as we think they are without taking the time to drill down into the gray areas and really think through them.

‑⁄ı∖‑

Conclusion

My life experiences in the years after that college class in which the professor asked, "What is your philosophy of life?" have allowed me to answer his question at last. When I contemplate all the inflection points in my life, I can see in this rear-view mirror how they cumulatively created my personal view of life, or my personal philosophy.

I believe that adults are largely, but not always, a reflection of their lives as children. Those early experiences and the environment in which they take place set the stage for a personal understanding of what and how life works. This understanding can be positive, or it can, unfortunately, lead to a dystopian view of the world. But these early influences, as powerful as they are, are not immutable. They can be overcome, for better or worse, through later experiences.

I have a strong work ethic that has helped immensely in achieving my goals in life. I attribute the seeds of this ethic being planted by the adults in my early life. I believe things worked for are appreciated much more than things given that require no effort to achieve.

I believe that people are inherently good with exceptions. I strive to appreciate people for who they are, not what they appear to be. And I try to understand what people are attempting to convey when

I listen to them rather than getting hung up on the literal words of their speech.

I believe in the Golden Rule: treating others as I wish to be treated. This seems so basic, but it's far too often forgotten in interactions with others in society. In the stress of ordinary living and working, it is easy for people to lose themselves in being the star of their own movie while ignoring the feelings of others.

Family is important but many miss that value and support by not recognizing its worth. Keeping family ties strong takes effort, just as with maintaining many other aspects of life. There are disagreements, sometimes serious ones, that can cause lapses of communication for years but, in the end, it is important to work at keeping family relationships as good as they can be throughout life.

The wonderful, natural environment humans live in is unforgiving and must be viewed in that sense. The natural environment on this planet that allowed humans to evolve is one that must be maintained if humanity is to continue to exist. There are many people who do not understand this basic fact and their actions put all in peril of extinction. I believe that humans do many things to the earth they depend on for existence just because they can or they are easy, not because they are the right things to do for the long term. I am human, to be sure.

Creative expression is vital for progress in life. I love *Star Trek's* Vulcan salute, "Live long and prosper." To do so involves successfully adapting to changing circumstances. Creativity is necessary to simply meet life's survival challenges, but a creative mind also finds ways to nourish the soul. Creative pursuits that enhance the quality of life beyond simple survival can be found in the arts, literature, sports, exploring the natural environment, social interactions of all kinds, and mindfulness of all that is rich and nourishing around me and the world.

Having integrity and a sense of personal honor are crucially important for maintaining a positive feeling of self-worth. Life abounds with challenges testing my integrity. Some of the decisions I make in facing these challenges are contrary to the opinions of others and can be painful, but necessary, to maintain my sense of self-worth.

Greed, ego, and guilt are very powerful emotions that are useful to a degree but extremely destructive if carried to extremes. I recognize that emotions trump reason in many human interactions and decisions. I know that is true of myself, so I strive to keep a balance between emotions and reason. Sometimes I succeed and sometimes I don't, but I am conscious of the need to be aware of the role each play in decisions I make.

Exposure to other parts of the world and other cultures foreign to my own is important to me in realizing my full potential. I see this as crucial for achieving a state of enlightenment.

There is a false perception that humanity is divided into multiple races. Yes, there are different cultures, different skin colors, and other differences, both subtle and extreme, but we are all human and share the same basic desire for survival and to live a good life. There are differences but we are the entire human race, and so it is important to treat each other as such.

When I was in military training, one of the goals of the instructors was to show trainees they were capable of doing far more than they thought they could. This notion, now sharpened by experience, that when pressed, I am able to do more than I think I can, is important to me in developing a full life.

In a spiritual sense, I believe in a Higher Power that I am continuing to learn about. Experiences in my life have opened my eyes to a spiritual realm that I could not fathom at an earlier age, the age when I was first asked the question about my philosophy of life. I still do not comprehend the totality of a spiritual realm—and I probably never will—but I am comforted by my belief that there is *something* there. My sincere hope is that I will continue to appreciate the life I have been given, accept it for what it is, and when the end comes be thankful for the time I have been given.

Humans cannot seem to avoid war, and it is a tragedy. War, or the prospect of war, being reality, compels a nation to be vigilant and prepared. I believe every individual faces a choice when called to serve our country. If our nation is at peril, its citizens should do their part in its defense. To do otherwise risks the loss of the freedoms and way of life offered in this country.

All of this taken together has endowed me with a growing sense of enlightenment, a sense that I have made good progress in pushing back the darkness of ignorance with the light of understanding. This, then, is my personal philosophy of life.

—)｜(—

Acknowledgements

I HAVE BEEN FORTUNATE TO BE around many interesting and influential people in my life, many of whom I mention in this book. The most significant people in my childhood were my parents, Gwen and Bill Merck, my aunt and uncle, Gerri and Ernie Demcheck, and my grandparents, Alma and Lowry Keefe. While writing and focusing on my upbringing, I became consciously aware of the exceptional impact Grandfather Keefe had on shaping my view of life, a man I spent considerable quality time with in those early years.

My wife, Ksenia, who listened to my stories and lived through many of them with me, shared her insightful views and constructive comments in our daily conversations. These helped add clarity to my thoughts as I wrote.

Invaluable counsel in morphing my manuscript into a finished product was provided by a fabulous editor, Jain Lemos. Thank you, Jain.

~/|\~

About the Author

WILLIAM "BILL" F. MERCK II EXAMINES the life experiences that influenced his view of the world. This examination, he believes, will spark an interest in others to contemplate how their lives are shaped by their own personal experiences, particularly those from the formative childhood years.

Bill's philosophy of life began taking shape while growing up in a small town in South Georgia. These oftentimes indirect early lessons and influences became more obvious in later years while living with and meeting people from different cultures throughout the United States and Europe. His experiences in higher education, the military, government, and the private sector contributed to his ever-expanding perspective on life through interactions with people from all occupations and levels of society.

His first book, *So, You Want to Be a Leader: Secrets of a Lifetime of Success*, a guide for navigating the corporate world, is followed by *Breadcrumbs: Finding a Philosophy of Life*, an introspective dive into answering a question posed to him while in college: "What is your philosophy of life?"

He and his wife, Ksenia, live in Florida and spend time in Arizona.